"Anna Chesner and her colleagues have created a dynamic, lucid and far-reaching presentation of one-to-one psychodrama stemming from decades of innovative work at the London Centre for Psychodrama. The book is wonderfully reader-friendly and the illustrations are very special in terms of both creativity and utility. Many of the perspectives and practices featured here are also likely to be of interest to psychotherapists and counsellors who do not (yet) use psychodrama as an element within their clinical approach. I expect a standing ovation from within the field of psychodrama itself."

– Andrew Samuels, Professor of Analytical Psychology, University of Essex, UK

"This book is an exciting, generous and much-needed contribution to the field of psychodrama psychotherapy – essential reading for practitioners and students. It shows how healing and richly creative one-to-one psychodrama psychotherapy can be. Anna Chesner has brought together a group of international authors who range from the most experienced to the newly minted; all of them offer fresh ideas drawn from front-line one-to-one practice. The ideas are intellectually far-reaching and bold, and the case studies are empathic, humane and deeply rooted in theory and practice wisdom. Read this book and be inspired to develop your one-to-one practice to the next level."

– Dr Clark Baim, Senior Trainer in Psychodrama Psychotherapy (UKCP, BPA), Honorary President of the British Psychodrama Association, Director of the Birmingham Institute for Psychodrama, UK

"This is a remarkable book. It takes us on a guided journey through the application of psychodrama in the one-to-one therapeutic context. Theory appears in measurable doses without diverting the main path. We pass through several examples of practice and careful explanations show us the reason that various decisions are made. Techniques of doubling, role reversal, de-rolling, coaching and more are carefully explained, and the reader can visualise the practical session. This is the genius of the author, her capacity to bring alive her work in a genuine and real way. One quotation must suffice to illustrate: 'a two-part role relationship can be worked on without actually taking on the role of the other. It is worth remembering that the role relationship exists not only as a historical experience and narrative but also as an internal object relationship.' I found this book immensely readable, informative and accessible."

– Professor Sue Jennings PhD, Professor of Play (EFD), visiting Professor University of Derby, UK, Specialist in Neuro-Dramatic-Play (www.ndpltd.org)

One-to-One Psychodrama Psychotherapy

One-to-One Psychodrama Psychotherapy: Applications and Technique will be an invaluable resource and manual to the field for those training in or practising psychodrama psychotherapy in a one-to-one frame. This book brings together for the first time current thinking and practice, developed and refined at the London Centre for Psychodrama Group and Individual Psychotherapy.

Divided in two parts, this book provides a comprehensive background to the field and an exploration of the theory and techniques discussed, drawing upon the experience of practitioners in their one-to-one practice. Case studies are presented and discussed across diverse issues, such as anxiety, bereavement, shame, eating disorders, dissociative identity disorder, multi-agency work with children and brief interventions within an organisational setting.

One-to-One Psychodrama Psychotherapy will appeal to all experienced practitioners as well as those wishing to work with psychodrama psychotherapy on an individual basis.

Anna Chesner is a UK Council for Psychotherapy-registered psychodrama and group analytic psychotherapist and creative supervisor. She has trained arts therapists, integrative counsellors and psychotherapists, and is Co-Director of the London Centre for Psychodrama Group and Individual Psychotherapy. She has written extensively on dramatherapy, psychodrama psychotherapy and creative supervision.

One-to-One Psychodrama Psychotherapy

Applications and Technique

Edited by Anna Chesner

LONDON AND NEW YORK

First published 2019
by Routledge
2 Park Square, Milton Park, Abingdon, Oxon OX14 4RN

and by Routledge
52 Vanderbilt Avenue, New York, NY 10017

Routledge is an imprint of the Taylor & Francis Group, an informa business

© 2019 selection and editorial matter, Anna Chesner; individual chapters, the contributors

The right of Anna Chesner to be identified as the author of the editorial material, and of the authors for their individual chapters, has been asserted in accordance with sections 77 and 78 of the Copyright, Designs and Patents Act 1988.

All rights reserved. No part of this book may be reprinted or reproduced or utilised in any form or by any electronic, mechanical, or other means, now known or hereafter invented, including photocopying and recording, or in any information storage or retrieval system, without permission in writing from the publishers.

Trademark notice: Product or corporate names may be trademarks or registered trademarks, and are used only for identification and explanation without intent to infringe.

British Library Cataloguing-in-Publication Data
A catalogue record for this book is available from the British Library

Library of Congress Cataloging-in-Publication Data
Names: Chesner, Anna, editor.
Title: One-to-one psychodrama psychotherapy : applications and technique / edited by Anna Chesner.
Description: Abingdon, Oxon ; New York, NY : Routledge, 2019. | Includes bibliographical references and index.
Identifiers: LCCN 2019004475| ISBN 9781138305700 (hardback : alk. paper) | ISBN 9781138305724 (pbk. : alk. paper) | ISBN 9780203728765 (ebk)
Subjects: | MESH: Psychodrama—methods
Classification: LCC RC489.P7 | NLM WM 430.5.P8 | DDC 616.89/1523—dc23
LC record available at https://lccn.loc.gov/2019004475

ISBN: 978-1-138-30570-0 (hbk)
ISBN: 978-1-138-30572-4 (pbk)
ISBN: 978-0-203-72876-5 (ebk)

Typeset in Times New Roman
by Swales & Willis, Exeter, Devon, UK

Contents

List of figures	ix
List of contributors	x
Acknowledgements	xiii

Introduction	1

PART I
Setting the scene   **5**

1	Framing creativity ANNA CHESNER	7
2	Role theory and role analysis: the bedrock of one-to-one psychodramatic work JINNIE JEFFERIES	19
3	Concretisation and playing with perspective ANNA CHESNER	31
4	Working with role ANNA CHESNER	51
5	Working with addictions: the addictions compass and intergenerational action genogram ANNA CHESNER	68
6	Psychodramatic dream work ANNA CHESNER	80

viii Contents

PART II
Case studies: the method in action   **91**

7   Understanding the child's voice: a systemic approach to
    one-to-one psychodrama psychotherapy   93
    PAULA DAVIES

8   Our deepest pain: working with shame in individual
    psychodrama psychotherapy   105
    ANNA NAPIER

9   Working with grief and loss   119
    LYDIA MAK

10 Working psychodramatically with anxiety   130
    VIRGINIE BOURY

11 One-to-one psychodrama with eating disorders   141
    EVA KOUMPLI

12 Lucy and her secret inner world   156
    ESTHER TANG

13 A brief one-to-one session using role analysis and role theory in
    a corporate organisation   169
    MAXINE DANIELS

    Index   182

Figures

1.1	Comparison of journeys	13
1.2	Typical session structure	14
3.1	Concretisation to find a focus	34
3.2	Action area for small world	35
3.3	Small world concretisation	36
3.4	Peter facing his boss	38
3.5	Peter's past impacting his present	40
3.6	Encounter with father	41
3.7	Encounter with anxiety	42
3.8	Developing a new internal role	43
3.9	Small world concretisation of a timeline	44
3.10	Maya's relationship	47
3.11	Maya develops a new role	49
4.1	Role taking and interview in role	54
4.2	Paul's encounter with mother	57
4.3	Role and mirror – working with multiple perspectives	64
4.4	Working with the double	66
5.1	The addictions compass	70
5.2	Intergenerational addictions action genogram	74
9.1	Sue's timeline	127
10.1	Oliver's sculpt	138

Contributors

Andrea Blair, MA, Dip Creative Supervision, is an artist and integrative arts psychotherapist and supervisor with a private practice in south-east London. She also works as an educational consultant in special educational needs (SEN) and social, emotional and mental health, advising schools, facilitating a mental health leads network and delivering training on SEN, wellbeing and youth mental health first aid. She embraces creative approaches in both her consulting and therapeutic work.

Virginie Boury, MA, is a dramatherapist and psychodrama psychotherapist with experience working with groups and individuals in psychiatric units, day services, therapeutic communities and private practice. At the time of writing, Virginie was in the process of completing her training at the London Centre for Psychodrama.

Anna Chesner, MA, is Co-Director of the London Centre for Psychodrama Group and Individual Psychotherapy. She is a UK Council for Psychotherapy-registered psychodrama psychotherapist and supervisor, working mostly in private practice in London. She has a passion for supervision and training, and runs the Humanistic and Integrative Psychotherapy College-recognised cross-professional creative supervision training at the London Centre for Psychodrama. She is widely published in the fields of psychodrama and action methods, dramatherapy and supervision.

Maxine Daniels is a UK Council for Psychotherapy-registered psychodrama psychotherapist with a BSc (Hons), Certificate of Education, Postgraduate Diploma in Psychodrama Psychotherapy and a Doctorate in Psychotherapy by Professional Studies. Maxine works as a consultant psychotherapist and clinical supervisor in hospitals for the Elysium Group, Priory Group and Broadmoor Hospital, where she uses psychodrama techniques to underpin her work. Maxine is an associate with Petros, a not-for-profit organisation delivering resilience training and coaching for staff within education, criminal justice agencies, health and corporate clients. She has presented at both national and international conferences on her work within the justice system with sexual offenders and is well published in the field. She is an academic advisor for the Doctorate in Psychotherapy by Professional Studies and a module leader for the Advance Practice for the Doctorate in Counselling Psychology and Psychotherapy at Metanoia Institute, London. Maxine is currently a senior trainer with the London Centre for Psychodrama.

Paula Davies is a qualified dramatherapist and group and individual psychodrama psychotherapist. She completed her psychodrama training at the London Centre of Psychodrama. In 1999, she was part of a small team of creative arts therapists bringing therapy into primary schools in Plymouth. She continues to work within the Plymouth Excellence Cluster, working with children and families in schools and homes. Here, she works as part of a multi-agency team and facilitates training for school staff as well as other professionals within the organisation. Paula also leads a multi-family group, supporting families where one or both parents have a mental illness through the charity Ourtime.

Jinnie Jefferies is a UK Council for Psychotherapy-registered psychodrama psychotherapist and the founding director of the London Centre for Psychodrama Group and Individual Psychotherapy. She is also Head of Psychodrama at Her Majesty's Prison Grendon Underwood, and in 2008 Princess Anne presented Jinnie with the Terry Waite Butler Trust Award for "outstanding work with long-term prisoners". She is the lead trainer for the Home Office training for those who work in therapeutic communities. In addition to her psychotherapy and training roles, she has written about her work and made television programmes on psychodrama and was recently involved in the BBC documentary *The Gun*.

Eva Koumpli is a UK Council for Psychotherapy-accredited psychodrama psychotherapist working with individuals, couples, groups and families in her Central London clinic. She is the founder and Clinical Director of the Tree of Life Clinic, which offers specialist therapeutic services for trauma, eating disorders, sex and relationship issues. Prior to setting up the Tree of Life Clinic, she was the Clinical Director of an eating disorders clinic in London. Eva has applied psychodrama in the prison service, the NHS, charities and addiction treatment centres. Eva's clinical and research interests lie in the areas of trauma, sexuality, gender issues and eating disorders. Eva qualified as a psychodrama psychotherapist first and then as a clinical supervisor at the London Centre for Psychodrama, Group and Individual Psychotherapy. She is currently receiving further training in psychosexual therapy.

Lydia Mak, MSc, MA, is a registered social worker living and working in Hong Kong. Her clinical experience includes the fields of trauma, depression and anxiety, offender rehabilitation, drug addiction and family work.

She gained her post-graduate Diploma in Psychodrama in Hong Kong in the London Centre for Psychodrama approach.

Anna Napier has 20 years of experience in the field of mental health as a group and individual therapist and supervisor. Initially she worked in the NHS as an occupational therapist before qualifying at the London Centre for Psychodrama as a psychodrama psychotherapist in 2009. She worked for several years in an intensive psychosocial day service for people with personality disorders. She is also trained in mentalisation-based therapy. She now works primarily in private practice in Central London as a psychodrama psychotherapist and supervisor, working with groups, individuals and couples.

Esther Tang, BA Psychology, Master of Social Work, has been a social worker in Hong Kong working in the field of schools, children and youth mental health services. She has applied creative methods and play in her work with children and youth. In recent years, she has been training as a psychodrama psychotherapist in the London Centre for Psychodrama approach. She has been running groups with young adults and parents struggling with mood and anxiety disorders.

Acknowledgements

I would like to thank the students at the London Centre for Psychodrama Group and Individual Psychotherapy for the privilege of learning from their learning process, and for their enthusiasm for the project of this book.

Acknowledgements also to my European psychodrama colleagues who have generously shared their writings and thoughts with me over the years. In particular, thanks to Roger Schaller from Switzerland, Elke Frohn and Ulf Klein from Germany, and to the community of psychodrama trainers who meet together annually for stimulating dialogue at the FEPTO (Federation of European Psychodrama Training Organisations) meeting.

Thanks to Marcia Karp for introducing me to psychodrama in an unforgettable way in the early 1980s, and to Jinnie Jefferies and James Bamber for their diligent and inspiring training and supervision.

Thanks to Andrea Blair for her sensitive engagement with the process of collaborating on the illustrations to my chapters.

Thanks to Rene Marineau and Ed Schreiber for their help locating references.

Thanks also to Dr Sandra Reeve for generously giving her time to read and reflect on my chapters.

Last but by no means least, thanks to the many clients whose therapy process has inspired both my chapters and those of the other contributors to this book.

Introduction

The idea for this book grew out of training sessions in one-to-one psychodrama as part of the group and individual training offered at the London Centre for Psychodrama. I have developed and led this module of teaching for over a decade, and found it both stimulating and revelatory to teach about what I have been doing in my practice for many years. At the same time, it became clear that there was no English-language book that represented and articulated our approach to this work. The trainees themselves pointed out the need for such a book and encouraged me to go ahead with it.

All the contributors in Part II have been trained in the London Centre for Psychodrama approach, whether in London or in Hong Kong. I decided to include contributions from both experienced and newly qualified practitioners and also those who are in the process of completing their training as the book is being prepared. There are two contributors from Hong Kong who have been part of the first two cohorts of the full psychodrama psychotherapy training there, set up by Jinnie Jefferies and myself in 2011.

What has kept me engaged in the art and profession of psychotherapy over the years is the fact that it is a practice through which I keep on learning, from the clients, and also from trainees and supervisees. This book is not intended as the final word on the subject. It is hoped that it will contribute to a dialogue, reflection and critical thinking about what we do as psychodrama psychotherapists working with clients in one-to-one therapy.

There are numerous psychodrama colleagues in the UK who would have much to share about their one-to-one practice. I chose to limit the contributions to those who have trained in the London Centre for Psychodrama approach. The range of experience is broad. Jinnie Jefferies was one of the two co-founders of the London Centre training in Psychodrama and Group Analytic Psychotherapy (with group analyst and Jungian analyst James Bamber), whilst others are in the final stages of their training nearly thirty years later. My hope is that the reader will find some level of coherence of approach, whilst also witnessing the individuality, cultural diversity and unique clinical experience of each writer's voice.

This book is divided into two parts. Part I is devoted to setting the scene, both in terms of psychodramatic thinking and the rich array of tools for creative action that psychodrama psychotherapists can use. Chapter 1 is about the underlying philosophy of psychodrama, and the interplay between this philosophy and the frame of one-to-one psychotherapy. It opens up some relevant questions about time, pace, frame and touch. Chapter 2 is contributed by Jinnie Jefferies, who focuses on role theory, an important body of theory that links closely to the philosophical base of psychodrama as well as to the London Centre for Psychodrama's role analysis approach. She introduces the history of role theory, and discusses the contribution of a number of theorists in this field. In Chapters 3 and 4 I explore psychodramatic technique, in particular the use of concretisation and role. In Chapters 5 and 6 I give a brief introduction to specific techniques developed for working with addictions and with dream. Throughout these chapters I share numerous vignettes of practical work done with clients, often creating composite clients for illustration purposes, so that the reader can "see" the method in action, as well as read about the thinking behind it.

A note about the illustrations: psychodrama is based on the mantra "show me, don't tell me". I have collaborated with art psychotherapist and educational consultant Andrea Blair to show visually some of the concepts introduced in Part I of the book. Other authors have also included photographic illustrations in their chapters.

Part II introduces the reader to a number of practitioners drawing upon these approaches in their one-to-one practice. These case studies cover diverse presenting issues, such as anxiety, bereavement, shame, eating disorders, dissociative identity disorder, multi-agency work with children, and brief interventions within an organisational setting. Paula Davies in Chapter 7 explores her multi-agency work within a school setting, where role analysis contributes to a shared language amongst the adults engaged with supporting children at school over time. In Chapter 8 Anna Napier tackles the arena of shame, focusing on her work with a variety of different clients in private practice for whom shame is a key theme, albeit presented in different ways. She shares her judicial use of psychodramatic interventions and role analytic thinking. The theme of shame also follows us into Chapter 9, where Lydia Mak opens up cultural perspectives as she engages with the issue of grief and loss in her Hong Kong psychodrama practice through an exploration of her work with one particular client with multiple bereavements.

Virginie Boury in Chapter 10 approaches the theme of anxiety. Her case study brings this painful issue into a new perspective by focusing on the importance of the development of spontaneity in the client, and the gradual emergence of the healthy internal role of the initiator.

In Chapter 11 Eva Koumpli draws on her specialist multi-disciplinary experience in the field of eating disorders, and shares her work with a sufferer of diabulimia, supported both by her understanding of trauma theory as well as role analysis.

In Chapter 12 Esther Tang takes us again to Hong Kong, where she describes her work with a client who suffers from a form of dissociative identity disorder. She takes us through her process of working with this client across different therapeutic frames, from short-term group to individual psychotherapy, and then to a long-term group. Her chapter raises questions about the challenge of working with a method that in some way mirrors the dissociative defence of her client.

Dr Maxine Daniels in Chapter 13 takes us into a corporate environment, where she applies role analysis and psychodramatic technique within a one-off drop-in session to support staff members in processing the impact of a crisis situation.

We all invite you to journey with us through these diverse applications of the psychodrama method.

Anna Chesner, October 2018

Part I

Setting the scene

Chapter 1

Framing creativity

Anna Chesner

Creativity and spontaneity

The central philosophical concepts in psychodrama as developed by J. L. Moreno are creativity and spontaneity. These twin forces are deeply connected with each other. Spontaneity is the way of being that drives creativity and allows it to emerge. The opposite of spontaneity is being stuck in what Moreno terms a "cultural conserve" (Moreno, 1940, in Fox 1987, p. 46). Moreno depicts a cycle of spontaneity and creativity that leads sometimes, through habit, to cultural conserves and at other times, through a process of "warm-up" or inner preparation, to an increase in spontaneity and the breakthrough of lived creativity.

Psychodrama theory distinguishes between impulsiveness, which is a state of being driven by impulses without reflection, and true spontaneity, which includes elements of reflection and personal choice in the moment. There are strong connections between this state of being and mindfulness, another discipline which integrates sensory, mental and physical elements with an emphasis on moment-to-moment awareness.

Psychodrama psychotherapy rests on the principle that human beings in their true nature have access to creativity and the capacity to be in the moment, spontaneously meeting the world with what it presents to the best of our ability in any moment. We can assess our state of well-being and fulfilment in life in terms of the degree of creativity and spontaneity in our lived experience. This impacts our relationship with self, other and the world.

The importance of warm-up is well known by athletes, musicians, dancers, artists and theatre practitioners. Moreno takes the concept into everyday life. All creative acts emerge through a process of warm-up, an internal and external preparation for a state of spontaneity and readiness, out of which something surprising and fresh can arise.

As a theatre-based model of psychotherapy, psychodrama thinks about the human being in terms of role, understood as a way of being, or "the functioning form an individual takes" (Moreno, 1961 in Fox 1987, p. 62).

Encounter

Despite the theatrical base of psychodrama, great emphasis is placed on authenticity and the concept of encounter. Moreno's poem *Invitation to an Encounter* describes this with visceral directness:

> A meeting of two: eye to eye, face to face.
> And when you are near,
> I will tear your eyes out
> And place them instead of mine,
> And you will tear my eyes out
> And will place them instead of yours,
> Then I will look at you with your eyes
> And you will look at me with mine
> (Moreno, 1915, p. 2)

There is an affinity between the work of Moreno and his contemporary Martin Buber, whose philosophy of dialogue and the distinction between the I-thou and I-it relationship fit well with psychodrama. In both philosophies we find an existential world view and a celebration of the person-to-person authentic encounter. Already in 1914 Moreno, in his pamphlet *Invitation to an Encounter*, describes the encounter in terms of a meeting of two in silence, a look or a conversation. I quote it here in the original German:

> Das heilige Feuer, das diese Schrift atmet, ist die Einladung zu einer Begegnung. Auf Gasse oder Markt, im Garten oder Gemach: wo auch immer mein Antlitz und das deine aufgeht, bereiten wir uns zu einem Schweigen oder zu einem Blickwerfen oder zu einem Gespräch.
> (Moreno, 1914, p. 5)

Here Moreno invites the reader to three aspects of the encounter: a silence, a glance, a conversation. The verbal conversation is mentioned third of these three kinds of encounter, and this reflects Moreno's interest in the embodied and non-verbal domain. This early poetry is a powerful evocation of the philosophy that underpins psychodrama as it developed throughout Moreno's life.

Expressionism

The style of Moreno's early writings and the rawness of his ideas place him within the Viennese expressionist movement. The quality of intensity that characterises this style of theatre and art is recognisable within the method of psychodrama, even as it has developed since then. As a movement, it favoured the expression of the inner world of the artist, through bold strokes and colours, and represented a socially critical world view, embracing the depiction of the dark side of humanity and society. One of the founders of Expressionism, Ernst Ludwig Kirchner, wrote:

> With faith in progress and in a new generation of creators and spectators we call together all youth. As youth, we carry the future and want to create for ourselves freedom of life and of movement against the long-established older forces. Everyone who reproduces that which drives him to creation with directness and authenticity belongs to us.
>
> (Kirchner, 1906, as quoted in Dempsey, 2010, p. 74)

These words of Kirchner are very much within the tradition and spirit of Moreno's thought.

The philosophy of psychodrama, and of the related disciplines of sociometry and sociodrama, is holistic. Moreno's aim, expressed perhaps in a grandiose but also truly visionary way, was to have "no less an objective than the whole of mankind" (Moreno, 1978, p. 3). What is important about this in terms of the philosophical underpinnings of the method today is that the lens through which the work is viewed is not limited to the inner world of the individual, nor even to their interpersonal world, but embraces the wider field, including the social and even transpersonal domains. As a cosmic being, man is a creator, and, like Prometheus, has access to the creative powers traditionally attributed to the gods. In Moreno's poem above he begins by evoking the sacred fire, "das heilige Feuer". Greek mythology tells us of the creative power of Prometheus, who stole fire from the gods. Moreno was a man with a Promethean vision, with a belief in mankind's right to fulfil our creative potential. We need to be reflective about how we handle that fire.

Frame in psychotherapy

Let us begin by considering the importance of the frame in general in psychotherapy. This refers to the conditions surrounding the interpersonal dialogue between client and therapist. These conditions are explored, explained and contracted for at the outset of a therapeutic relationship. They include factors such as location, time, duration and frequency of sessions, whether the work is time limited or open-ended, face-to-face or using online or phone technology, fees and methods of payment where relevant, cancellation policies, and an understanding of confidentiality and its limits. There may be further factors such as procedures for contact between sessions, or for risk management.

The frame provides clarity around mutual expectations, predictability, and a protected space for psychological work that allows for and respects the vulnerability inherent in the endeavour of psychotherapy. The psychotherapeutic relationship is bound to be asymmetrical to some extent – both parties are there to focus on the client's rather than the therapist's needs, and the therapist is there by virtue of some expertise in the field. The therapist may also gain self-knowledge, learning and a degree of transformation through the work, but this is not the primary purpose of the sessions. This asymmetry being a given, the frame itself is honoured by both parties and is intended to serve the work. In psychodramatic language the frame provides a degree of role clarity for all involved. While the psychotherapeutic journey tends to be a journey into the unknown, or half-known, the frame offers an important element of the known.

The frame provides an essential container for emergent processes. It may at times be resented, attacked, ignored or renegotiated. The way a therapist holds the frame and the way a client adheres to it or struggles with it both reflect something significant about our way of being in the world.

Psychotherapy emerged out of psychoanalysis, and the typical frame in that setting would be multiple sessions per week of 50 minutes duration, with the analyst aiming to be a blank screen, neutral and abstinent from taking any action, in order to allow the transference to develop and be worked through. In modern psychotherapy in the UK the frequency is more likely to be weekly or twice a week with a similar session length. Some therapists offer a 60-minute session rather than a 50-minute session. The "talking cure" sits comfortably within that kind of time frame.

Does this time frame also suit psychodrama psychotherapy and other action or arts-based approaches? Are we trying to fit a quart into a pint pot, or in Morenian terms, are we unquestioningly buying into a "cultural conserve" which will limit the spontaneity and creativity potential of the work? Each practitioner must engage with that question for themselves. For my part, I see the frame as a discipline offering form, within which there is the potential for creative freedom.

Some psychodrama colleagues use a 60-minute or 90-minute frame in order to allow more time to accommodate an action intervention. These are legitimate choices that can be justified in terms of the time required to warm up to a piece of action, to engage with it, de-role it and reflect on it together. However, my experience is that a 50-minute session is adequate as long as the therapist does not over-complicate the action intervention offered and paces the work mindfully and with attunement to the client, within the time frame available.

Rhythm and pace in group psychodrama psychotherapy and in one-to-one psychodrama psychotherapy

Psychodrama was developed predominantly as a group method, and it is only in the past fifteen years that the UK psychodrama psychotherapy trainings have explicitly taught the method as a one-to-one practice alongside group psychotherapy. It is helpful to reflect on the pace and rhythm of these contrasting settings for the clients, how these impact on the therapeutic process, and how therapists need to adapt their own pacing with this in mind.

A typical group session is two and a half hours long, beginning with a check-in and warm-up, moving on to a protagonist selection, contracting for the particular piece of work, then the main action phase, whether focusing on a one-scene vignette or a multiple-scene classical psychodrama, and finally a sharing in which the group members de-role, give role feedback and engage with their personal resonances with the work. It is an intense journey in which the internal world of the protagonist is made visible on the psychodramatic stage. Interpersonal relationships are thus scrutinised in action, and linked with early experiences that were key turning points in the creation of meaning for the protagonist, and the development of patterns of relating that have since become outdated and problematic. Role analysis is used to clarify the context-specific response to particular situations, the feelings and behaviours evoked by the context, and the underlying unconscious beliefs or assumptive world that drive current behaviours and ways of being. There is an opportunity to view the early (locus) scene from outside (the mirror position) and intervene in a way that revises the meaning that was internalised at that time. The final scene is an opportunity to practise a new way of being (role training) as the first step towards integration of the work and the manifestation of creative change.

The classical way of depicting the therapeutic journey of a group psychodrama session is a spiral, one that begins on the periphery and works its way towards the centre and back out to the periphery. The spiral image captures succinctly the time travel involved in classical psychodrama, from the present to the past and back to the present (for multiple examples of this process, see Goldman and Morrison, 1984).

How does this translate into the one-to-one setting? The group psychodrama psychotherapy process is quite a journey in terms of depth and intensity, both for the protagonist and the group. Moreno used the analogy of having surgery, in that the protagonist needs time "post-operatively" to integrate the work, for the work to process them.

As a group process, one piece of work tends to evoke memories and issues for other group members, who are encouraged to articulate these resonances in the first instance during the sharing and to work on these themselves in due course within the group. In practical terms this means that each individual is unlikely to be the protagonist for two or more sessions in a row. There may be circumstances where this does happen, but in general the focus tends to move from one individual in the group to another, each one holding the group concern on that occasion. For the individual in the group this means that the perspective and intensity will vary from week to week; one week they may be the focus of the group's support and explore a personal issue in depth, another week they will have the opportunity to play roles for another group member, or simply to view the main part of the action from the position of audience or witness. Playing a role for another group member or viewing a psychodrama from the position of audience can both function as a warm-up to personal material and provide a new perspective on personal issues that may already have been worked on in the group. There is a complexity of process, which allows for integration of personal work done in the group whilst the group focus moves to another individual in the group, or onto group-as-a-whole processes.

In one-to-one psychotherapy the client is always the focus. This does not mean that they are always the protagonist, in the sense of actively working through action on a personal theme. There may be sessions that are reflective only, a time for integration or for sharing. (Sharing in this sense refers to a dialogical phase of the therapy process, and not the structured ritual whereby a protagonist in a group, who has revealed much of themselves, gets to hear about the resonances and identifications from the life of group members.) Other sessions may function more as a warm-up for a future focus in the work. Some sessions may be the equivalent of a vignette, or a one-scene piece of work from a group psychodrama session. From time to time there may be a process that is closely analogous to a group session, in connecting present and past patterns through a process of role analysis.

If classical group psychodrama is best depicted as a spiral, then a one-to-one psychodrama psychotherapy process can be symbolised by various distinctive threads of narrative that flow forward in an apparent tangle (Figure 1.1). Sometimes one, sometimes another thread is prominent, sometimes they overlap, diverge or come together. In a single session there may be a focus on a particular thread, a particular point of coming together of a number of threads, or reflecting at a meta level on the journey so far.

There is an arc of intensity in a group psychodrama that leads to the locus work, often accompanied by an emotional catharsis about two thirds of the way through the session. In one-to-one work the arc of intensity stretches over weeks or months, reaching an organic climax from time to time when there is a "breakthrough moment" at a level of emotion or insight. It is essential for the practitioner with a background in classical group psychodrama psychotherapy to appreciate this difference, and to develop the personal and professional role flexibility to adapt to the frame. While a group session is like a feast of many courses, which requires time to digest, the one-to-one frame offers regular bite-sized therapeutic nourishment. To use an analogy from film and TV, a group psychodrama is more like the immersive experience

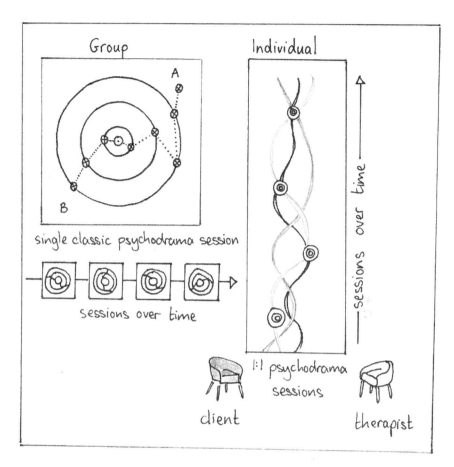

Figure 1.1 Comparison of journeys

of a film, while one-to-one psychodrama psychotherapy functions more like a long-running TV serial, whereby several threads or plot lines are opened and from week to week the focus may be on one or another of these threads.

The arc of a session in one-to-one psychodrama psychotherapy is less defined than in a group session. Some practitioners may follow a familiar process of warm-up, action and closure for each session. The London Centre model favours a more psychodynamic approach, in which the themes of the session tend to emerge through free-floating dialogue at the start of the session, during which the therapist notices the possibility for action interventions (see Figure 1.2). At some point an exploration in action may be offered. The timing of any action intervention is crucial, in that therapists need to calculate and manage the level of complexity and emotional impact of this intervention

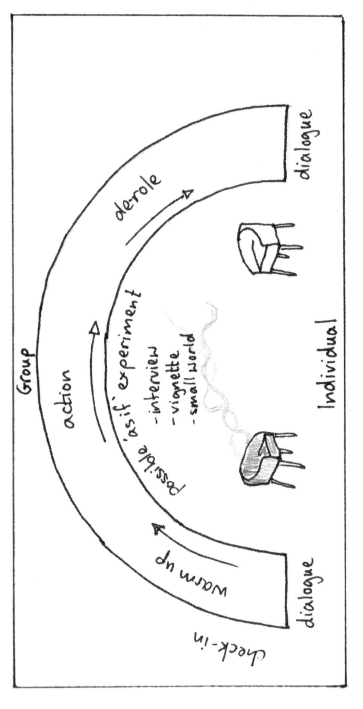

Figure 1.2 Typical session structure

in terms of their responsibility to prepare safely for the end of the session. The principle here is that what is opened up needs time to be de-roled, cleared away and reflected upon within the session. If the key opportunity for action emerges quite late in the session, it may be wiser to simply name the possible psychodramatic work and return to it in a subsequent session. Alternatively, it may be viable to do a short and simple action intervention with the possibility of a further in-depth exploration at a later point.

The main principles here are safety and consent: consent in the sense that moving into creative action tends to bring out more unconscious or pre-conscious material, and the client needs to be part of the decision as to whether this an appropriate moment for such work. We have the responsibility not to overwhelm a client with material that is highly emotional when there is inadequate time to process it within the session.

Linked to the question of timing is the recognition that we are not aiming to complete the kind of working through that is possible in a classical group psychodrama session. Working through happens in a different way in the one-to-one setting, over a longer period of time. We have to create closure of any action intervention within the session. If therapists put themselves under pressure to approach the work in terms of directing a number of scenes within one session, this is probably an indication that they are getting caught in the classical group session structure as a cultural conserve. It may be that they are overly concerned with their own performance as therapist rather than holding the client's process over time. The quality of being with the client is at least as important as any kind of doing that we may initiate.

Touch

Touch needs to be thought about carefully in terms of the frame in one-to-one psychodrama psychotherapy. In traditional verbal psychotherapy there is a clear norm that there is no physical contact within the session. Depending on cultural factors, there may be a ritualised handshake at the start or end of a session. It is usual to negotiate different norms around touch amongst experiential and physically oriented psychotherapies, such as dance movement psychotherapy and body psychotherapy. As an embodied experiential psychotherapy, psychodrama as practised in a group usually does involve touch, which helps both with emotional regulation and with experiential warm-up to the material. I shall name here three examples of the ways in which touch is legitimately normalised as part of the process and form in group psychodrama psychotherapy.

Firstly, we often see the therapist/director holding the protagonist's hand whilst pacing together and talking during the contracting stage or during the transitions from one scene to the next. At this point the director might be sharing their role analysis or formulation of the work so far. It is an effective tool for preparing to enter the "as if" of a scene. The bilateral rhythmic stimulation of walking in a circle seems to aid attunement between therapist and protagonist, and to foster a state of reflection and dialogue at the same time as allowing an internal exploration on the part of the protagonist, through which important memories may emerge which will influence the next scene. Another example of the use of touch in group psychodrama psychotherapy is in the use of the double, whether embodied by a group member as auxiliary or, from time to time, by the director. The close physical attunement of the double, in which breathing, body posture and thought processes are shared, is a subtly powerful and intimate form of communication in which the I-thou of the encounter gives way to an I-I relationship, through which the doubles offer themselves as an extension of the protagonist's ego, helping them stay grounded in the room or helping them articulate what is felt but hard to put into words. Thirdly, we often use physical closeness and holding within a childhood scene and also at times within the group as a form of sharing and connecting on a person-to-person or group-as-a-whole level. As a protagonist re-integrates the role of their inner frightened or distressed child, the group method offers the opportunity of a physical reaching out, embracing and sharing of a new message of soothing or acceptance. This is done through the use of role and role reversal. For example, the adult protagonist role reaches out to their own inner wounded child on the stage, and experiences both giving and receiving that reparative hug through role reversal.

Should this norm be carried into the one-to-one frame? What is at stake if we do or do not include moments of touch and physical closeness in the work? Each practitioner needs to engage critically with these questions. Undoubtedly the choice is relationship-specific, and norms of engagement can be specifically contracted for and consented to within the sessions on a case-by-case basis and in response to any given moment in the therapeutic process. For myself, as a rule of thumb I avoid touch within the one-to-one frame, which means finding other ways of doubling, and other ways of attuning and supporting at times of emotional dysregulation or dissociation. Why do I position myself at that end of the continuum of touch/ abstinence from touch? Firstly, there is an undeniable asymmetry of power in the therapeutic relationship, and I would rather err on the side of caution than risk a casual assumption that it is safe and feels safe for the client. The nature of the therapeutic relationship positions the therapist unavoidably to some extent as the expert, and therefore the one who knows best and the one who sets the norms of the frame, so there is a risk that discomfort on the part of the client could be overlooked, by both therapist and client. Secondly, there is a clear and predictable ritual frame in group psychodrama, so moments when there is likely to be physical contact are known by the group members, can be negotiated explicitly, and crucially, are witnessed by the group. In the one-to-one frame there are no witnesses and there may be different connotations to touch in a one-to-one situation.

Factors that may influence how we position ourselves in relation to this question are space, culture and gender. Working in a generously sized studio space invites a more experimental physicality in which proximity and movement can more easily be part of the exploration, while working in a more domestically sized consulting room allows less freedom to negotiate proximity non-verbally and evokes more domestic or familiar associations around proximity and touch. The question of culture is multi-layered: there is the culture of psychotherapy, the culture of psychodrama, the culture and history of the two individuals in the room. As for gender, this is an area that relates to both power and sexuality, and needs special consideration, especially in light of the transferential dimension of the therapeutic relationship.

How do we bring the benefits and power of the method into the work if we take a more abstinent position in relation to touch than we would in a group setting? Some other options for helping with affect regulation in the one-to-one setting include offering a blanket to place on the shoulders of a distressed client, whereby the sense of touch comes from the blanket rather than the therapist's hand; or encouraging the client to hold a cushion or teddy bear as a soothing sensory intervention; or facilitating mindful breath work at times of heightened emotional arousal.

The adaptation of the familiar psychodrama techniques to the one-to-one frame is explored in some depth in Chapters 3–5 as well as in the case studies that form Part II of the book.

Psychodrama as a way of thinking

Is it still psychodrama psychotherapy if there is no action component in the session? Arguably yes, there is a choice to use or not use action in a session. Including action by habit may be just as much a cultural conserve as never using action in a session. Psychodrama psychotherapy is not uniquely about techniques, exciting though they may be. It is just as much about a philosophical base centred in the value of creativity – spontaneity in everyday life, and an extensive theory of role as developed by J. L. Moreno (in Fox, 1987); Z. Moreno (2015), Clayton (1994), Bustos (1994), Williams (1989), Daniel (2007) and others. Role analysis offers a tool for listening and making sense of multiple narratives. Going back to the image used above of a tangled stream of threads as a concretised depiction of the complexity of interwoven narratives that often emerge in one-to-one psychotherapy, role analysis is a way of understanding, formulating and navigating this complexity. It is a method of listening and reflecting that can be immensely supportive to verbal counsellors and psychotherapists from other disciplines, who may find themselves wondering how to make sense of the free-flowing narratives that emerge in their work. As a way of listening and thinking, it is supportive of what Donald Schön (1991) calls "reflection in action", the capacity to think critically about what we are doing while we are in the process of doing it.

The role theories mentioned above, as well as the London Centre approach to role analysis, are written about in the next chapter by Jinnie Jefferies, the co-founder, with group analyst James Bamber, of the original London Centre for Psychodrama and Group Analytic Psychotherapy in 1990. In Chapters 3–6 I write about psychodrama techniques and how they can be adapted both to the one-to-one frame and to address particular therapeutic issues. The case studies in Part II of the book give examples of how psychodrama psychotherapists and senior trainees have used both role analysis and a variety of techniques from psychodrama to work with their one-to-one clients in different settings.

References

Bustos, D. (1994). Wings and Roots. In P. Holmes, M. Karp, M. Watson (eds.), *Psychodrama Since Moreno*. Routledge.

Clayton, M. (1994). Role Theory and Its Clinical Application in Practice. In P. Holmes, M. Karp, M. Watson (eds.), *Psychodrama Since Moreno*. Routledge.

Daniel, S. (2007). Psychodrama, Role Theory and the Cultural Atom: New Developments in Role Theory. In C. Baim, J. Burmeister, M. Maciel (eds.), *Psychodrama Advances in Theory and Practice*. Routledge.

A. Dempsey (ed.) (2010). *Styles, Schools and Movements: The Essential Encyclopaedic Guide to Modern Art*. Thames and Hudson.

Goldman, E. E. & Morrison, D. S. (1984). *Psychodrama: Experience and Process*. Kendall/Hunt.

Moreno, J. L. (1914). In R. Waldl (ed.) (2005), *J.L. Morenos Einfluss auf Martin Bubers Ich und Du*. [online www.waldl.com/downloads/Waldl_Morenos_Einfluss_auf_Bubers_Ich_und_Du.pdf]

Moreno, J. L. (1915). *Einladung zu Einer Begegnung, Bericht von Jacob Levy*. Anzengruber Verlag Brüder Suschilzky.

Moreno, J. L. (1940). Spontaneity and Catharsis. In J. Fox (ed.) (1987) *The Essential Moreno: Writings on Psychodrama, Group Method, and Spontaneity*. Springer.

Moreno, J. L. (1961). The Role Concept: A Bridge between Psychiatry and Sociology. In J. Fox (ed.) (1987), *The Essential Moreno: Writings on Psychodrama, Group Method, and Spontaneity*. Springer.

Moreno, J. L. (1978). *Who Shall Survive?* (3rd ed.). Beacon House.

Moreno, Z. (2015). *The Quintessential Zerka*. Routledge.

Schön, D. (1991). *The Reflective Practitioner*. Routledge.

Williams, A. (1989). *The Passionate Technique: Strategic Psychodrama with Individuals, Families and Groups*. Routledge.

Chapter 2

Role theory and role analysis
The bedrock of one-to-one psychodramatic work

Jinnie Jefferies

Central to the understanding of psychodrama as a treatment method is the theory of role. Fox (1987, p. 62) defined Moreno's concept of role "as the actual and tangible forms which the self takes and it is the symbolic representation of this form, perceived by the individual and others that is called role". In this chapter I will trace the history of role theory, define Moreno's definition and contribution to role theory and acknowledge the contributions of other psychodramatists in the field, and finally describe the approach adopted by the London Centre for Psychodrama Group and Individual Psychotherapy which informs the practice of the one-to-one contributors to this book.

History of role theory

In their chapter entitled "The Nature of Role Theory", Biddle and Thomas (1966) traced the history and the development of role theory. They listed the names of about two dozen writers whose work appeared during the period 1890–1930. Those listed could be called the "precursors of role theory because their contribution to the perspective of role was prior to the emergence of a language and specialised inquiry into problems of role" (Kipper 1986, p. 7). The beginning of modern role theory is attributed to the works of the sociologist George Herbert Mead, published posthumously in 1934, Jacob Levy Moreno (1934) and Ralph Linton (1936). Mead focused on the social aspect of role in the development of the self. According to Mead, the self is not there from birth, but develops from social interactions and observations. The individual develops a self by role taking, the observation and internalisation of the opinions and feelings of the other. When these combine with the individual's response to such interactions, a self emerges

Moreno acknowledged the concept of role taking, which he described as "Being in life itself within its relatively coercive and imperative contexts" (Moreno 1953, p. 722), but added that the creation of role goes through two stages:

role perception which is cognitive and anticipates forthcoming responses and role enactment which is a skill performance. A high degree of role perception can be accompanied by a low skill for role enactment and vice versa. Role playing is a function of both role perception and role enactment.

(Fox 1987, p. 63)

Moreno described role playing as "The choice of playing a role in a chosen setting for the purpose of exploring, experimenting, developing, training or changing role" (Moreno 1953, p. 722).

Linton, an anthropologist, proposed a distinction between two concepts when considering role: "Ascribed Status", a socially assigned position, without reference to an individual's innate differences or abilities, and "Achieved Status", determined by an individual's performance or effort, role. This distinction implied that positions and attending roles are elements of societies and that the behaviour of an individual can be construed as a role performance (Linton 1936). Therefore role, according to Linton, is the link between individual behaviour and social structure. "In following decades, these ideas were further developed and investigated by other scientists, mostly sociologists and social psychologists. Historically however the notion of role did not evolve from sociology or psychology" (Kipper 1986, p. 7), but has a basis in theatre, as outlined below by Moreno.

Moreno's contributions

Moreno (1960, p. 80) described the development of role throughout the ages:

"Rôle", originally a French word which penetrated the English language is derived from the Latin word *rotula* (the little wheel or round log) on which sheets and parchments were fastened so as to smoothly roll (wheel) them around since otherwise the parchments would break and crumble. These sheets were assembled into a book like composite which subsequently came to mean an official volume of papers used in law courts.

The word "role" was part of English and European languages for many years, but it was not until the early 1920s that it started to be used in the behavioural and social sciences as a technical concept, and in the 1930s in the Americas the term was employed technically in writing on role problems (Kipper 1986, p. 7).

Moreno bridged the social and individual dynamics and saw the concept of role as a useful tool in therapy, group work and everyday life. His concept of role fitted well with his theories of sociometry, an instrument which measures human interactions within groups, and went beyond Mead and Linton's limited theories of role as a single social dimension. Psychodramatic role theory offers a bridge between social sciences and psychiatry, and is therefore more inclusive and carries the concept of role through all dimensions of life. For Moreno:

> a role is the functioning form an individual assumes in the specific moment he reacts to a specific situation in which other persons or objects are involved. The form is created by past experiences and the cultural pattern in which the individual lives. Every role is a fusion of private and collective parts.
>
> (Fox 1987, p. 62)

In developing his concept of role theory, Moreno saw individuals as role players who progressively add the roles necessary for their survival and create other roles out of their responsiveness to the environment. First, a set of private roles emerges: these are shaped by collective roles in the environment. These collective roles, such as the role of father or mother, define in some way how these roles should be performed. As the individual develops and meets new challenges, the number and kinds of roles they take continuously change. Some of these roles are adequate, productive and useful, and some are not. Other roles never develop. Moreno described this as an individual's role repertoire. The pattern and development of a person's repertoire of roles describes in part their personality (Starr 1977).

For Moreno there are four categories or basic types of roles:

- Somatic or Psychosomatic Roles – These roles include such activities as eating, sleeping, style of dress and social habits.
- Social Roles – These include occupational roles, economic class, racial, gender and family roles.
- Psychodramatic Roles – These can be described as fantasy roles or dreams or wishes of being or achieving something different in one's life, such as achieving a happy marriage, a successful career or becoming an adventurer. This category also includes all the characteristics of one's imagination, fictional figures, people in our memories or dreams, and complexities of attitudes and behaviours (Moreno 1966).

In addition to the types of roles, there is a range of ways in which the role can be performed. For example, the psychosomatic role of eater could be described as anorexic. The psychodramatic role of the wished-for role of adventurer could be described as fearless or cautious. Adding adjectives to the roles performed fleshes out the ways in which these roles are portrayed and might highlight the difficulties the individual encounters in their daily interactions with self and other. An individual in therapy may display a difficulty in the role or the way the role is performed. In real life, the individual is living within a complex comprised of many roles operating on several levels.

Another helpful concept Moreno introduced was that of "role reciprocity". Many of us feel that we are helpless in a given situation when involved with an other. We wait for their behaviour to change in order to realise our own happiness. What we fail to acknowledge is that if we change our own behaviour, it will result in a change in the other's behaviour. It may not result in the response we would desire, but at least we are no longer trapped in an unchanging situation. A wife or husband who suspects the other of having an extramarital affair waits for the relationship to end, feeling helpless until it does. However, if the situation is confronted rather than avoided, the other may choose to end the extramarital relationship or choose to end the marriage and make the affair permanent (not the desired response), but at least the role of helpless victim shifts. Psychodrama is governed by the principles of spontaneity and creativity. Moreno described spontaneity as:

> a new response to an old situation, rather than the same old stereotyped response and an adequate response to a new situation, rather than the inability to deal with something just because it is new and finally an adequate response to a combination of old and new.
>
> (Goldman & Morrison 1984, p. 6)

Therefore, role functioning can be perceived as requiring both spontaneity and creativity in order to achieve the appropriate response.

Other contributors to the concept of role theory

Blatner and Blatner

Adam and Allee Blatner (1988, p. 105) expand on the notion that roles are not fixed in time and suggest that in considering roles, the following principles need to be thought about:

- Roles can be learnt and be revised.
- Roles can be lost and taken away, relinquished.
- Roles can be modified and redefined.
- Most roles are implicit or explicit social contracts; they require an agreement by others to behave in some reciprocal fashion.
- Many roles exist in relationship to others; the role of son implies a parent.
- Conflicts or difficulties of adjustment often emerge as people engage in the dynamic process of changing aspects of their role – learning, redefining, renegotiating, or making transitions between major life roles.

Every relationship consists of many roles, and there are often conflicts among these roles. For example, a marriage includes such roles as sharing money, management, romance, social interests and child rearing. The conflict within these roles is built into the nature of most relationships.

Many roles have sub-roles or role components. Sometimes there are conflicts between these role components. A mother needs to protect her children yet encourage their risk taking. People usually have some conflicts among their various roles – a chef may plan a menu on the basis of both economic and aesthetic considerations.

Awareness of these dynamic factors, the range of roles and the different ways roles may be played become clues for diagnosis or clues for helping the therapist and the individual in therapy.

When an individual comes into therapy, the questions that need to be asked in relation to role theory are:

- Are some dimensions of the personality being suppressed, and is this in some way causing a problem for self and other?
- Are some roles expressing an excessive or distorted motivation?
- Can the essential need be recognised?
- Might roles expressing one facet of the personality be overdeveloped in part because others are being neglected?
- Are there important dimensions of personal development that are being repressed or denied, and could the client's actions express efforts to compensate for or disguise these needs? (Blatner & Blatner 1988, p. 106)

Max Clayton

Max Clayton brings another dimension to role theory. He views roles as being part of a Role System. Within the "Progressive and Functional Role Systems" roles are either well developed or in the process of developing. These roles show a person's ability to function and deal with difficult situations. A "Coping Role System" involves those roles which are moving towards being progressive and functional and those moving away and against this process. "Coping Roles" can be viewed as a temporary measure of dealing with a threatening situation in the absence of a more productive way of reacting. Finally, he describes a "Fragmenting Dysfunctional Role System". Within this system roles are diminishing or unchanging. Clayton advocates working with and enhancing "Progressive Roles" and developing these further. This results in the "Coping Role System" diminishing. For him stronger working links develop between the "Progressive" and "Fragmenting Role" systems, and as such fragmenting roles move from the unchanging category to the diminishing category. Unlike Williams and Bustos, Clayton does not choose to discover the locus of the roles he describes as "Fragmenting" and "Dysfunctional". Role training for him "aims to bring about the development of specific limited

24   Jinnie Jefferies

aspects of human functioning (role) so that a person's professional or personal goals are achieved more adequately" (Clayton 1994, p. 142). Therefore Clayton does not focus on a total personality reorganisation, which is the major intent in a classical psychodrama session. Instead his approach is more behavioural, strengthening "Progressive Roles" that already exist or are in the process of development.

A session would begin with a description of specific aspects of functioning that need attention. Then follows dramatic enactment of a relevant situation in which a role diagnosis is made, identifying those roles that are adequate, overdeveloped, conflicted and absent.

Antony Williams

Antony Williams developed Moreno's role theory further, introducing the importance of analysing a role into five components to enhance our understanding of the process. As a systemic therapist, Williams views role as being part of a system that involves self and others. He states: "a person's inner self is inextricably entwined with the selves of others and ... directors search as soon as possible for the transactional component of a role" (Williams 1989, p. 23). Strategic psychodrama focuses on the familial ties and loyalties that continue to influence role. As a child the client may have had little choice about the way in which these roles (ways of being) were carried out, either because they were too little to consider other ways of responding to life events or because of the physical and emotional power of the adult world surrounding the child. The child's response to an abusive, violent parent may offer little alternative but to suppress one's voice and simply find a way of surviving the ordeal. However, the continuance of these roles into adult life presents even more of a problem, but one that can be amenable to new experiences through the psychodrama process. For Williams, the goal of a psychodrama is for the individual to develop a more functional role system and to bring that system into contact with their old role system: "A strategic psychodrama approach aims to promote new definitions in the system that will lead to rapid and durable changes in the functioning self" (Williams 1989, p. 23).

For Williams, role does not exist in isolation. Therefore it is essential the therapist consider the *context* of the role that is to be explored. Bateson (1979) noted that the context of role reveals how the reactions of an individual to the reactions of other individuals are organised by time: "Investigating the context of role implies an initial enquiry about what the other members of the social atom do and say when the protagonist is in a given scene" (Williams 1989, p. 59). What Williams is saying here is that a person's behavioural response (way of being) is not static, but is influenced by the reactions of the other, be it person or situation. Roles are not permanent, and if the individual attempts to fixedly maintain that role from one context to another,

Role theory and role analysis   25

they and those around them can experience considerable distress. Context and time are highly significant in determining what the appropriate response should be. The role of a nurturing mother needs to be very different than when that same mother, as a chair of her company, deals with industrial issues. Or similarly, when faced with an employee's recent bereavement, she will need, as chair of the company, to take a very much more sympathetic approach. It is not the time to be assertive or conflictive.

In understanding role defined by context, there are for Williams four other components to consider. Having established a *contract* as to which role system needs to be addressed, the therapist has to investigate the *behavioural response* – the individual's reactions. This focuses on not only what the individual does and says, but also what they do not say or do. Detailed information about behaviour can reveal important distortions or contradictions that are key to understanding the systemic functioning of the client's behaviour. When using action methods in one-to-one therapy, the therapist can profit by slowly enquiring about events leading up to, during and after the problem, as well as the attempted solutions.

The third component of role focuses on *the feelings* that are evoked by the reactions of the other and have a part to play in the individual's behaviour. Feeling hurt or rejected can lead to an angry outburst or withdrawal by the client.

Perhaps the most important component of role is the fourth component, that of the *belief system*. An individual's beliefs about self, the other and the world in which the individual co-exists shape and motivate the individual's behaviour and reactions. The psychodrama psychotherapist needs to find out what are the personal constructs of the client and who have been the main protagonists in steering the client in a particular direction, doing and saying one thing and not another, believing this and not that. If our client has a history of a significant other breaking or abusing their trust, their relationships with others are going to be at best based on caution and suspicion, and at worst relationships will be avoided at all costs.

The fifth component is that of *consequences*. Roles are designed to have an effect even though this cannot be predicted. Often the consequences of a role only become clear when one observes the outcome. It is important for the client to be made aware of the consequences of their response.

Dalmiro Bustos

This leads us onto the work of Dalmiro Bustos, an Argentinian psychodrama psychotherapist, whose origins lie in psychoanalysis. He brought to Moreno's theory of role a further perspective, clarifying the use of Moreno's terms "status nascendi", the moment in which something, in this case role, occurs, and "locus or matrix of role", the place where the role comes into being. Bustos was interested in the conditioning factors that caused/cause the individual to respond in a particular way. This is similar to Williams' belief component of role. For Bustos, when a patient comes for a consultation about a specific complaint, the therapist needs to consider the following:

1. a clear specific determination about what is wrong and what has to be put right;
2. an investigation of the locus or group of conditioning factors where this something was created (role);
3. an investigation of the specific determining response that the person made to the stimuli that were present (matrix of role);
4. an investigation of the specific moment when the response emerged (status nascendi) (Bustos 1994, p. 64).

By tracking the locus of role the therapist is able to understand the conditioning factors that existed when the role came into existence. Obviously a child's age is a defining factor, as already explained in reflecting on Williams' contributions. The parent's response, implied and explicit messages as to how to respond and the consequences of responding in a particular way are also important. The child may be a witness to what happens if one responds in a certain way, and whether there is a supportive other in the child's environment who might offer a different perspective or a "secure base" is also a contributory factor in understanding the original role response.

All of these factors – the child's age, the parent's response, the consequences of responding in a particular way and whether there is a supportive other in the child's environment – will determine the child's response.

Bustos, like Williams, has a systemic approach to the understanding of human suffering, and developed Moreno's concepts of roles which tend to form in clusters and the interactional state of roles (Moreno & Moreno 1977). For Bustos there are three main role clusters:

- Cluster One – to incorporate passively and to depend;
- Cluster Two – to look for what we want, to achieve autonomy;
- Cluster Three – to share, compete and rival.

Cluster One: As individuals, we know that to be able to love as an adult we need to depend maturely on the person we love. Life from time to time creates its own frustrations and losses. It is at these times that we need to allow ourselves to be cared for and supported, to be passive and dependent.

Cluster Two: This refers to those roles that bring autonomy and independence. In this cluster the roles which involve work, self-confidence, and the capacity to achieve and exercise power will be active.

Cluster Three: Focuses on the roles of friendship and companionship. They are collegiate and fraternal, and involve competing, sharing and rivalry. According to Bustos, these roles help us create limits on others' behaviour; they help us take care of possessions and defend against attacks of aggression.

Roles in these clusters are either symmetric, in that the complimentary roles have the same hierarchy with the same rules applying to both parties, or asymmetric, in that the power is clearly handled by one of the two persons involved. The usefulness of these concepts enables the therapist to understand the dynamics of their patient. Which are the preserved roles? Which are the roles most affected? Which are the functions that need retraining? An individual may have difficulty in one or more of these role clusters: for example, clients may have difficulty in allowing themselves to be cared for by others or seeking out support, or being autonomous and achieving their goals, or competing or defending themselves against personal attacks (Bustos 1994).

The London Centre approach

The London Centre for Psychodrama Group and Individual Psychotherapy has adopted, amalgamated and adapted the teaching of both Williams and Bustos to provide a working structure for the group and individual therapist.

At the beginning of a piece of psychodramatic work the therapist will establish a contract. What will be the focus of the session? What is the problem? What needs to change? Setting a contract enables the therapist to stay on track, and any material that is introduced will need to relate to the contract, to define what is relevant and to discard that which is not. In individual and group psychotherapy the therapist will ask the client to recall a situation that demonstrates or identifies the problem, asking such questions as: "Where are we?" "What happens?" "Who else is involved?" "Who starts the action?"

Whilst listening to the story (maybe shown through action using small world figures or re-enactment of the problem using auxiliaries in group psychodrama), the individual and group therapist identify the role structure:

Context: The situation or circumstances that cause the client to behave in the way they do. Is it perceived rejection, humiliation etc.?

Behaviour: What does the client do and not do when presented with a set of circumstance that involves other people and holds memory traces of past relationships?

Affect: What are the client's feelings about the interaction?

Belief system: What is the client's underlying belief system that drives or motivates the behavioural response? The why of our reactions is all-important.

Consequences: What is the effect on our client and the other when our client chooses to respond in a particular way?

Having established an analysis of role, the therapist and client will find it useful to explore whether, when the client is faced with a similar context where the situation is similar but the content or persons involved are different, the client responds in the same way. This insight can be revealing to the client, for so often we believe that our problems lie with a particular person rather than a situation, and that if we can change the person involved, the problem will go away. How many people divorce and find a new partner only to find the same problems emerge over time when similar conflicts occur?

Having identified the role structure (Williams' five components of role) and made a Role Analysis, the therapist will identify conditioning factors that led to the belief system that drives the behavioural response in a given situation (Bustos' locus of role). This will take the client and therapist back to early childhood, where their beliefs about self, others and the world they inhabit were established. It may be that having experienced a similar situation in childhood (Bustos' "status nascendi"), the client was reprimanded, punished, even beaten for their response, and so they learnt to suppress their feelings and their voice and hence in the present situation simply accept their fate. It may be that they were a witness to what happened to others when they stood up to an authority figure, and as such vicariously learnt not to repeat such actions themselves. Or they may have identified with the behaviour of others and made it their own. How often does a client acknowledge in the process of therapy that they are responding just like their parent responded? Our past shapes our present, and as such needs to be attended to when the past has scarred our present way of being (role).

Arriving at this place, the locus of role, and having identified the conditioning factors, the therapist must now make an intervention. Whilst acknowledging that at the time the client had little alternative but to accept the messages given, the therapist must now challenge and deconstruct the dysfunctional belief systems that continue to hinder their client's role response to a given situation. Once aware of their process, the client will need to address those who set up the dysfunctional belief system. This may result in an expression of anger, or tears, or finding a voice to say what was needed at the time but not given. Of equal importance is the need for client to give themselves a different message and permission to behave and react in a different way in a given situation, and as such change the belief system that has hitherto activated the behavioural response. For the client and the therapist this is an intense and emotional stage of the therapy. Later chapters in this book will demonstrate how this is done using action techniques.

It is important to remember that Moreno's existential approach would see each moment in which the individual responds (role) shot through with memory traces from the past as well as anxieties about present and future possibilities. His emphasis was on the present and the future. An understanding of our past was for Moreno only important in order to change our present way of functioning. It is therefore essential, having understood the process by which we respond to a given situation, to have an opportunity within a session to practice a different response. This takes us to the concept of role training: "Role training, in contrast to role playing [which focuses on the exploration of the external and internal nature of role formation], is an effort, through the rehearsal of roles, to perform adequately in future situations" (Fox 1987, p. 63). Moreno saw psychodrama as a laboratory for practising living. The London Centre for Psychodrama emphasises the importance of providing an opportunity to practise new ways of being, practising new roles. For both the group and individual therapist this will entail reflecting with the client on what has been learnt and what needs to change and how this change will take place. This could simply result in a reminder to self or a conversation with the significant other.

There is an ordered simplicity in the psychodrama process. In working with the protagonist, we:

- begin with the present problem;
- find similarities in the recent past;
- discover the linkages in the deep past;
- achieve a catharsis if necessary;
- concretise the issues, choices and actions that keep the client in the present dysfunctional state;
- help the client see their options in life;
- aid in the integration of the cognitive and affective;
- achieve closure and healing so that the client can carry out in life what has been learned in therapy (Goldman & Morrison 1984).

The above process is enriched by our use of and understanding of Moreno's role theory.

Conclusion

An understanding of the richness of role theory and its application enriches and enhances the work of therapists from a variety of disciplines and can aid those who choose to work in the one-to-one frame. It informs and directs the interventions that are made.

References

Bateson, G. (1979). *Mind and Nature: A Necessary Unity*. Bantam Books: New York.
Biddle, B.J. & Thomas, E.J. (1966). The Nature of Role Theory. In *Role Theory: Concepts and Research*. Wiley & Sons: New York.

Blatner, A. & Blatner, A. (1988). *Foundations of Psychodrama History, Theory and Practice*, 3rd edn. Springer: New York.

Bustos, D. (1994). Wings and Roots. In *Psychodrama Since Moreno*, edited by P. Holmes, M. Karp & M. Watson. Routledge: London.

Clayton, M. (1994). Role Theory and Its Clinical Application in Practice. In *Psychodrama Since Moreno*, edited by P. Holmes, M. Karp & M. Watson. Routledge: London.

Fox, J. (1987). *The Essential Moreno: Writings on Psychodrama, Group Method, and Spontaneity.* Springer: New York.

Goldman, E.E. & Morrison, D.S. (1984). *Psychodrama: Experience and Process.* Kendall/Hunt: Dubuque, IA.

Kipper, D.A. (1986). *Psychotherapy through Clinical Role Playing.* Brunner/Mazel: New York.

Linton, R. (1936). *The Study of Man.* Appleton-Century: New York.

Mead, G.H. (1934). *Mind, Self and Society.* University of Chicago Press: Chicago, IL.

Moreno, J.L. (1934). *Who Shall Survive?* Beacon House: Beacon, NY.

Moreno, J.L. (1953). *Who Shall Survive?* 2nd edn. Beacon House: Beacon, NY.

Moreno, J.L. (ed.) (1960). *The Sociometry Reader.* Free Press: Glencoe, IL.

Moreno, J.L. (1966). Psychiatry of the twentieth century: function of the universalia; time, space, reality and cosmos. *Group Psychotherapy* 1, 1946–1958.

Moreno, J.L. & Moreno, Z.T. (1977). *Psychodrama*, vol. 1, 4th edn. Beacon House: Beacon, NY.

Starr, A. (1977). *Psychodrama: Rehearsal for Living.* Nelson-Hall: Chicago, IL.

Williams, A. (1989). *The Passionate Technique.* Routledge: London.

Chapter 3

Concretisation and playing with perspective

Anna Chesner

Winnicott writes in *Playing and Reality* that "psychotherapy takes place in the overlap of two areas of playing, that of the patient and that of the therapist. Psychotherapy has to do with two people playing together" (Winnicott 1971, p. 44).

In this and the following chapter I begin to explore the core techniques of psychodrama and reflect on their use in one-to-one work as ways of bringing an element of play into the therapeutic process. Brief examples are given, based on an amalgamation of various pieces of client work. The main technique explored in this chapter is concretisation, through which elements of role and mirroring come into play, while in the next chapter the focus is more directly on role as a technique.

Concretisation

A core feature of psychodrama is that we give concrete form to what otherwise may be experienced as elusive and internal. We put "out there" what is otherwise inside, as is highlighted in the title of Paul Holmes' (1992) book on psychodrama and object relations theory, *The Inner World Outside*. Why make things concrete? As Kafka writes: "my attention strays too easily when there is nothing there to put one's finger on" (Kafka 1913, p. 207, in Frohn and Klein 2016). Kafka's statement refers to his struggle to read a philosophical book, but the same principle is true for many people when trying to make sense of life and experience. By placing the inner world outside, our internal and relational worlds become more tangible. This facilitates our ability to reflect on these worlds. We can literally put our finger on things which may otherwise be hard to grasp.

Therefore, concretisation as a technique is about giving concrete form to situations or dynamics that would otherwise be expressed abstractly, in words. These dynamics may be interpersonal, systemic or intrapsychic. The concretised image inhabits a third or liminal space (see Van Gennep 1961; Winnicott 1971), from where it is viewed together by therapist and client. It can be explored piece by piece or as a whole. It can be viewed from different perspectives (literally and metaphorically) by moving it or moving around it. It can be described as it is, or transformed into a future possibility, for example something desired or feared. It can be augmented by as yet absent or underdeveloped roles. It can be played with, and as Winnicott reminds us, this is the essence of psychotherapy.

As a technique, concretisation requires a stage or action area, whether small or large, and an audience or spectator position, which relates to the function of the observing ego. The interplay between these two spaces and ways of being is a distinctive feature of the method in the one-to-one setting and can be profoundly therapeutic in its own right.

Following the core principle of psychodrama of "Show me, don't tell me!", I now share some examples, together with some reflections on the value and purpose of the method used. We begin by diving straight in to the early part of a session.

Vignette 1: concretisation to find a focus

CLIENT CATHERINE: I don't know where to begin, there is so much going on.

THERAPIST: Here is a pile of cushions, different colours, textures, designs. Let's name the themes you have mentioned, and you choose a cushion to designate that theme and lay it on the floor, wherever feels right to you.

CATHERINE: Well, as I said, there's my not sleeping well. Here, this soft and fluffy cushion can be the sleep that I'm missing. Then there's that argument I had with my partner ... this red one should do, I'm so angry about him coming home late again. And then I'm worried about my children, I want to protect them from our arguments ... these two cushions are really lovely, one for Peter, one for Poppy. Let's put them side by side.

THERAPIST: And what about something to represent the issue we began to explore last week, about the new job you were applying for?

CATHERINE: Oh yes, well that's really receded into the background with all the relationship stuff going on – this golden cushion would fit, it's such a dream job ... but it's way over there in the corner. I can't even think about it right now.

THERAPIST: So, looking at the spread of issues that's around today, where do we need to put our focus?

CATHERINE: The red cushion, I need to get my head around what's going on between me and my partner.

Commentary

In this example, the client selects and places the cushions, and in so doing finds her own way into prioritising where she will put her focus in the session. This happens quite spontaneously, because the action of choosing and placing the cushions engages less conscious, felt processes, and the visual impact of what is in front of her makes it very clear where her warm- up is. When there is a higher level of inhibition on the part of the client, I have initiated the concretisation myself, as a form of reflecting back what I have heard, and at the same time modelling that we can communicate by showing rather than telling. The client can then be asked to re-configure the cushions in a way that is more accurate for them (Figure 3.1).

Concretisation as small world

Miniatures can be used in a variety of ways within one-to-one psychodrama practice. As a general rule, it is advisable to determine a stage or action area for the work (Figure 3.2). This can be defined by laying out a piece of paper or cloth as coloured background, folded or moulded to a size and shape of the client's choosing. Other possibilities include the use of a communicube or communiwell (Casson 2007), both of which offer several layers of stage on a transparent plastic structure which allows multiple levels to be used and viewed simultaneously within a contained space. A sand tray offers a different kind of stage, one which enables the sensory experience of working with wet or dry sand that can be moulded and configured in three dimensions as a background to the miniatures. It allows the particular possibility of being able to include figures that are hidden or part-hidden as well as those that are visible. The use of sand trays exists also as a therapy in its own right, drawing on a Jungian base, as Sandplay Therapy (Turner 2005), as well as being used as a more generic approach in play therapy (Homeyer 2016). The psychodrama practitioner may usefully train in either of these specific methods to deepen their understanding of the potential of this medium and form. Alternatively, they may approach the sand tray with spontaneity as another form of "stage" for projective psychodramatic work.

Something quite hypnotic happens for most people when working with small world sculpts. There is a quality of absorption that is reminiscent of a child's projective play, or of the kind of creative attention familiar in artistic processes. I am reminded of the experience of walking along a beach with pebbles, stones and shells. Once we start to select some to take in our hand, we tend to scan what is in front of us, maybe picking some objects to hold and feel before establishing that they are "right" or can be discarded. It seems to me that we recognise when some object is a "match". Perhaps it is simply aesthetically pleasing, or maybe there is a recognition that the object mirrors an internal state. Most of us know this feeling from discovering the world through play as children. Arranging or playing with these found objects connects us to an artistic mode of self-expression that for many people comes easily.

The process of miniature object selection in the consulting room is usually a rather more guided one (Figure 3.3). The therapist may ask, "Choose an

Figure 3.1 Concretisation to find a focus

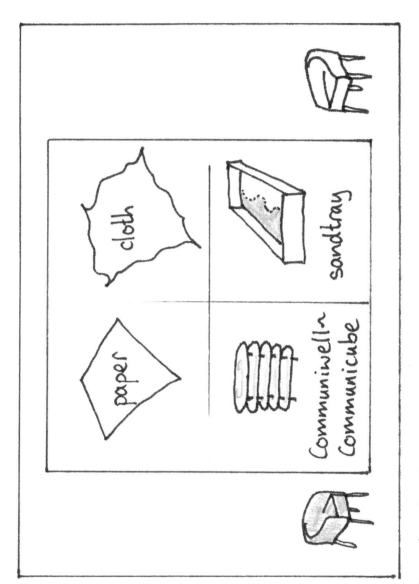

Figure 3.2 Action area for small world

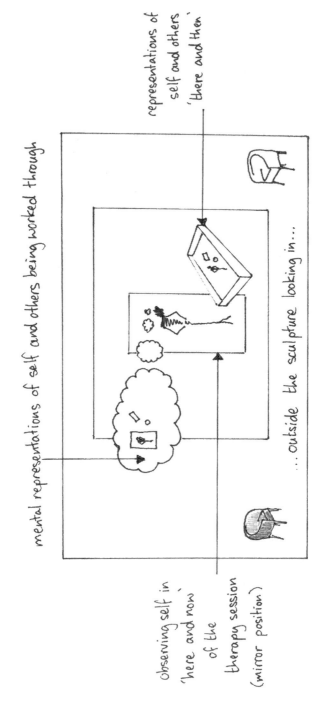

Figure 3.3 Small world concretisation

object to represent you in this situation we are discussing, and one for the other significant people." The client's choice of object to represent self, an aspect of self, other(s) or even abstract values invites a form of creative projection through which they invest a great deal of personal meaning into the objects. As the person handling and positioning the objects, the client is firstly a creator, sculptor or director of their piece. Once the different pieces are given their places, the client moves more into the observing or mirror position, which encourages reflection; immediate reflection on what has been sculpted, and also reflection on what it represents. The investment of meaning into the figures and their particular relationship with each other involves a deeply personal quality of absorption and identification, which is why the therapist usually refrains from touching the placed objects, which are at that point in role as part of the client's inner world. As a technique, its value contains a paradox: the relative scale of observer (large) and observed (small) is empowering and allows for aesthetic distance; the identification with the objects which have been chosen through unconscious or pre-conscious resonance brings a depth of involvement. Clients experience themselves as both inside the sculpture and outside the sculpture looking in.

Working through a transference of situation

When the therapist introduces role taking and role reversal as an added intervention in a small world sculpture, it is possible to benefit from multiple perspectives on the same situation, similar to what is possible in group psychodrama sessions. In the following example we see how a client, through showing a recent problematic situation, is able to unpack the historical scene behind it (analogous to locus work in classical group psychodrama). The presenting image can be understood in terms of transference of situation, whereby the role dynamics of a current situation evoke the emotional and behavioural response of an earlier formative situation. Through making the implicit beliefs about themselves and others explicit, clients find their way towards a significant shift in the present. We join the session at the point where the action part begins.

CLIENT PETER: This shy little boy figure with the football is me, and the monster towering over me is my anxiety. We are facing my line manager, that's the badger, and that's when the anxiety really kicks in.

THERAPIST: Is the monster there all the time?

CLIENT: No, just when my boss's attention is on me.

THERAPIST: Put your finger on the badger and speak as your line manager to you (indicating the little footballer).

CLIENT AS LINE MANAGER: Where's the report I asked you to do last week? I thought we agreed you would submit it this morning, no?

THERAPIST: Okay, now put your finger on the anxiety, the monster, and let's hear what the internal message is.
CLIENT AS ANXIETY: That's done it! You're useless and he knows it. He can see right through you! The writing's on the wall, you're gonna lose this job. Be afraid! You're stupid, useless, and now you're exposed.
THERAPIST: And now put your finger on little footballer you and let's hear what you think and what you say both to your boss and to your anxiety.
CLIENT AS SELF AT WORK: I feel small, I'm kind of frozen, I don't say anything much to my boss ... just "It's on its way" or something like that. And to my anxiety, it's more just a physical response, I go all shaky inside, and sort of agree with the message of anxiety: "Yes, I am useless, I can't kick the ball, can't deliver the goal." (Figure 3.4)

At this point in the work the scene includes an interpersonal element and an intrapsychic element. The piece of concretisation could finish here, with a reflection on the part of client and therapist on the situation that has been shown. The rest of the session would take the form of verbal dialogue. Alternatively, the concretised image can be regarded as a presenting scene, and the exploration could go further:

THERAPIST: We are looking here at your role response to being reminded by someone in authority, your boss, that you need to deliver something,

Figure 3.4 Peter facing his boss

Concretisation and playing with perspective   39

or perhaps that you are late in meeting an obligation, an expectation ... that is the context here. Your role response is maybe not so visible to your boss, in that you manage to say something about the piece of work being on its way. Internally it's a different story, you shake and your anxiety feels like a self-attacking monster, with a message that really undermines your confidence. It tells you that you can't deliver and that you are useless. That's what you believe about yourself in the moment. That in turn contributes to your feeling stuck, inadequate and alone. What I notice here is that you are not able to contact your own resources, or indeed ask for help. It's a stuck and really uncomfortable situation for you.

PETER: Absolutely!

THERAPIST: As you look at this little footballer figure standing in the shadow of this monster with its unhelpful and attacking messages, do you have a sense of who stands behind this figure?

Commentary

The framing of this question represents a turning point in the session. It is an invitation for the client to make links. The thinking behind the invitation is that a distorted and extreme response to a current or recent situation is likely to be transferential in its nature, and thereby offers a potential door into earlier significant memories.

CLIENT PETER: As I look at the image, the three of them, I see so many examples ... behind my boss would be my maths teacher at school, and that monster figure would absolutely be my father, and that little boy is me at about aged 11. My father was a scientist and was so impatient, I was such a disappointment to him when I couldn't get it right straight away. How strange, I knew something was being evoked from the past, but it's so clear looking at it!

THERAPIST: Let's make it even clearer. I invite you to choose a figure to stand behind the anxiety monster, something to represent your father as he was back then, and another figure to represent your teacher, standing behind your boss.

As Peter places a fox behind the badger to represent the teacher from his childhood and an owl behind the monster to represent his father, the double image formed shows two scenes superimposed on each other: the current situation and the formative situation in the "there and then". The similarity of his own role response between the two scenes is made visible and offers material for therapist and client to reflect on together (Figure 3.5).

Figure 3.5 Peter's past impacting his present

Commentary

At this point, there are three different time frames active in the room: the here and now of the reflective therapist and client, the recent scene of the situation at work, and the more distant formative or locus scene from childhood. The relative size of the concretised image in relation to the scale of the therapist and client in the here and now facilitates the reflective function and helps avoid the client being overwhelmed by too much material. As the next piece of verbatim material shows, the technique helps clients mentalise themselves and question their previously implicit assumptions or beliefs about themselves and others.

PETER: I can see why I chose the little footballer figure for me now: I feel as alone and shy and inadequate and young at work, as I did when I struggled at school. I'm reacting to my boss as if he were unapproachable. Actually, he's not, he'd probably give me a bit of guidance if I asked. But I don't let myself see or explore that potential for help, I'm so busy being at the mercy of that monster, dismissing myself, being impatient with myself, treating myself like my father did.

THERAPIST: What's the feeling you are in touch with right now, looking at this?

PETER: Anger! Something needs to change here. I want to tell my father to back off, and I want to tell my anxiety to get off my back. And I want to give myself a new message, something to help me be more in my strength, in my adult role.

THERAPIST: Go ahead, let's start with your message to father.

PETER: (with his finger on the little footballer figure, looking at the figure of the owl) Back off, dad, I don't want to be burdened by your sense of disappointment and frustration with me. If you can't be more helpful, just back off, back off! (Figure 3.6)

THERAPIST: Is there more?

PETER: Probably, but that's enough for now. I want to say something to my anxiety. I want to change it, shrink it … (removes the monster figure and replaces it with a smaller object, a spaniel). I need a more loyal internal message.

THERAPIST: Let's hear that new message, put your finger on the spaniel and speak the new message to Peter.

PETER AS SPANIEL: I'm with you, I know this is hard, but we can do it, I have faith in you and I stand by you. You can learn new things, of course you can.

THERAPIST: I hear the emotion in your voice and see how moving this new message is for you.

Figure 3.6 Encounter with father

PETER: Yes, it is, I need to practise this. It makes me feel warm and less alone, more like I can find my adult role (Figures 3.7 and 3.8).

The session continues with de-roling of the image and reflection on the important links made. Subsequent sessions reinforce the insights and emergent roles from this session. The idea of the internal spaniel becomes a shorthand for Peter's capacity to give himself a supportive internal message when faced with new challenges.

Small world concretisation of a timeline

Here the technique of concretisation is used to map out a sequence of some sort, perhaps key points on a lifeline, or something more focused such as the client's relationship history, addictions history, or history of losses and bereavement. For a concretised lifeline, a rope or long ribbon can be used as the line, with its ups and downs that the client can configure. Relevant people or moments are concretised with miniature figures, wooden blocks, shells and stones. These are placed in chronological sequence along the line, perhaps with the more positive ones on one side of the line and the more challenging ones on the other.

Once the image is created, the client can sit or stand and talk through the image. It acts as a prompt and as a representation of the narrative as

Figure 3.7 Encounter with anxiety

Figure 3.8 Developing a new internal role

a whole, which can be particularly helpful in terms of contextualising particular moments as part of a longer narrative. Patterns and sequences are made visible, which aids understanding both for the client and the therapist. The client can determine which events, encounters and relationships are particularly key, and these can be marked for further exploration at a future time (Figure 3.9).

The technique is simple in its structure, and the image can be reconstructed in subsequent sessions if new information has come into consciousness between sessions. The concretised narrative is thus seen as a developing process rather than a fixed thing.

The therapist can invite further exploration by inviting the client to play with their physical positioning in relation to the line. Australian psychodramatist Antony Williams developed a related technique called "Memory Lane" (Williams, personal communication) in which the client is asked to stand at the point in the timeline that represents the present moment. This creates a clear initial perspective of looking back through time and anchors the work in the present as a place to return to. The client can then be invited to the beginning of the timeline and to step along it, naming the memories that arise as they walk from the past towards the present moment.

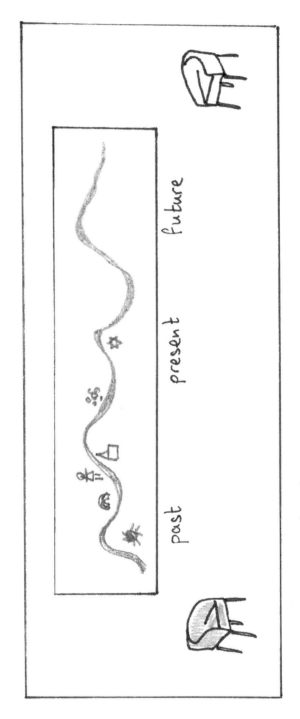

Figure 3.9 Small world concretisation of a timeline

Concretisation as family sculpt or social atom

Using miniatures to map out the client's current or historic family system can be a useful technique in the early stages of therapy or at times when there is interest in revisiting a particular moment in the client's history. The former works as a compact way of imparting a lot of basic historic information, and the image becomes the focal point for discussing relationships, family roles and culture. Distance, spatial relationship between objects and choice of object can be revealing and give an opportunity for the client to reflect on the different perspectives within the family system. The curiosity of the therapist can be expressed indirectly through the sculpt rather than as a list of questions that may be received as intrusive.

In the following excerpt a new client, Patti, is in her second session and introduces the therapist to the dynamics in her family when she was growing up. She has created a small world image of herself, her brother and her parents.

THERAPIST: I notice that you and your brother are standing together, and that your father stands behind you. Can you see him there from where you are (indicating the client figure in the sculpt)?

CLIENT PATTI: Actually, that's right, we don't see him, we didn't see him much. He was always so busy with work. The one we saw most was our nanny. She needs to be in the picture. Can I add her?

THERAPIST: Sure! Choose an object to represent her.

PATTI: (placing a relatively large peasant figure in the sculpt) There, now it is complete, she is right with us.

THERAPIST: And from here it looks like she stands directly between you and your father.

PATTI: Yes, she did all the practical things for us, but emotionally I would always want mother ... she's kind of between me and mum as well. Interesting, the way I've positioned it, my brother gets direct contact to mum, but I have to go around my nanny ... that fits, it's how it was.

Moreno developed the concepts of social atom and cultural atom as ways of mapping the relationship world of the client. They are techniques that can be drawn on the page or looked at in three dimensions. While in the example above concretisation in miniature gives client and therapist a chance to view a family system together, the invitation to create a social atom focuses on a broader question of "Who is in your life right now and where are you in relation to them?" This may include work colleagues, social, religious and political groups, as well as family of origin and current family networks. Clients choose a figure to represent themselves first of all, and position others or groups of others spatially in relation to themselves, not in terms of geographical distance, but in terms of emotional connectedness, closeness or significance, whether positively or negatively felt. The sculpt can include people who have died or left, and those with whom there is a conflictual relationship.

A useful way of understanding these concretised relationships is through the concept of *tele*, the Morenian theory of the positive, negative or neutral charge between people or groups (Moreno 1978). The client may be asked to indicate with their finger those relationships where there is a mutually positive tele – where they feel positive towards the other and it is reciprocated; where there is a mutually negative or conflictual tele – where they feel hostility, resentment, anger towards the other and the other towards the client; and where there is an asymmetric tele. In this case, while one party seeks closeness towards the other, the other seeks distance or is indifferent.

The exploration typically highlights relationship patterns and where the hotspots might be for the therapeutic work.

The method is particularly useful at the start of a therapy, as a form of assessment, and can be revisited from time to time as a means of reviewing change.

Concretisation and the creation of functional roles

Role is a way of being. Morenian and post-Morenian role theory gives us the opportunity to conceptualise our way of being in response to different circumstances in terms of spontaneity and creativity. Moreno defines spontaneity as "an adequate response to a new situation or a new response to an old situation" (Moreno 1978, p. 42). In the example of Peter above, we see him developing a new response to an old situation. In the example of Maya below, we see her facing a new situation and finding her way towards an adequate response. It is helpful to educate clients to regard role as a "way of being" and to introduce the idea that our personal role repertoire consists of some roles that are overdeveloped, some that are underdeveloped and others that are adequate. The implicit message in this concept is that we have the power to work on our way of being and to change it. The "I" is not a fixed and unchangeable entity, but a process in relation to the world around us. Concretisation can be used to facilitate work at a deep level, to change the role repertoire, or the balance of internal roles. In the example below, a young woman, Maya, is facing a new situation and finds her own language to empower herself.

The background to the session is that 20-year-old Maya, a young woman with a history of depression and self-harm, has recently had her first sexual encounter with a man (Guy), an event that was both a breakthrough for her and created a challenging roller-coaster of emotions. A few weeks on, she has discovered that he has been cheating on her.

CLIENT MAYA: I am struggling, I hate what has happened, I hate myself for still being attracted to him. He was the first person I slept with, and now

I find that he has lied to me, cheated, used me. I'm an idiot. It's my fault.

THERAPIST: It's a lot to process, isn't it? It was such a big step for you to sleep with him, and now you're confronted with yet another new situation. Let's take a look at the dynamics of this relationship together. I would like you to mark out a background or stage area with a cloth and to choose two to three objects to represent different aspects of you in this relationship, and two to three objects that represent different aspects of Guy.

MAYA: (lays out miniatures) OK, so that's him, the little figure with the smart clothes, that's his charm, his sense of humour and fun. Then there's the rabbit, that's his sexiness, he really likes sex! And then the fox, that's his wiliness. I think he's really cunning, sly, clever at relationships.

THERAPIST: And the two figures for you?

MAYA: I'm the little fairy, pretty naïve in terms of real relationships. And I'm this little kitten, friendly and curious, and affectionate. So just two figures for me.

THERAPIST: Show me what happens!

MAYA: (moves the kitten closer to the fox and rabbit and starts to cry) I know this relationship is bad for me, but I can't help it ... I know I'm getting hurt (Figure 3.10).

Figure 3.10 Maya's relationship

Commentary

At this point in the small world sculpt Maya has shown the situation as she perceives it and expresses her internal struggle through tears. She is in touch on the one hand with the excitement of the relationship and on the other hand with the pain it is causing her.

THERAPIST: Let's bring on a new role here. Can you choose an object from the shelves to represent the part of you that recognises this relationship is hurting you?

MAYA: (chooses a growling tiger) It's the tiger, they are fierce, protective and know how to survive. They are amazing animals.

THERAPIST: And where do you position this tiger part of you?

MAYA: (placing the tiger between the figures representing herself and those representing Guy) That changes everything!

THERAPIST: So what's tiger's message to Guy, and what's its message to you?

MAYA AS TIGER TO GUY: How dare you hurt Maya! (growls as tiger) I'm angry with you, you knew you were her first, you knew this meant a lot to her. You're selfish, self-centred, you're not what you seemed, and she deserves more respect!

THERAPIST: And tiger's message to you? (indicating the two aspects of Maya in the sculpt) Tell her!

MAYA AS TIGER: I'm here to help you learn how to survive. Listen to me. It was fine you slept with him, it was fine you trusted him, but now you know he has betrayed you, it is not fine any more. I'm here to tell you to break contact with him, to be careful. I know you are sexually attracted to him, but you are not someone who can be casual in relationships. You need someone more reliable. There are other possibilities out there, but for now give yourself some space, and do not get sucked in.

THERAPIST: Which part of you responds to this message?

MAYA: All of me. I agree, and I feel so much more powerful. It felt like he had all the power before, but now I can feel my own power, my inner tiger. There are times when I need to be fierce, maybe even with myself. Tigers don't let themselves become victims (Figure 3.11).

THERAPIST: Are you ready to de-role this sculpt?

MAYA: Yes, but I want to take my inner tiger with me.

Commentary

In this session, the empowering and protective role of the tiger represented a latent or undeveloped potential in the client. Once the figure of the tiger was found and placed in the sculpt, the client found it easy to access its words and its function. It is not always this easy to access or develop a new role, but in this case Maya found her spontaneity with relative ease through the medium of concretisation and role taking. The rest of the

Figure 3.11 Maya develops a new role

session was spent reflecting on how she could stay in touch with the power of this new role between sessions.

In terms of psychodramatic theory, the figure of the tiger belongs to the realm of surplus reality. It is a metaphor that carries over a potential quality of being from the world of nature into the inner world of the client and enables a new way of relating to herself and the other. It is a creative act on the part of the client to identify and concretise these qualities in a form that is accessible to her. As with Peter's spaniel, the role of the tiger is referred to in subsequent sessions as a shorthand for this developing capacity to face adult relationship challenges. In terms of role theory (Daniel 2007), we are looking here at a progressive and developing role, one that will need practice to fully integrate.

Conclusion

In this chapter I have shared examples of concretisation in one-to-one work. I see it as a flexible and accessible technique for gaining perspective and fostering creativity in the client. Having looked at some of the many possible applications of this method, and how it fits with role theory and role analysis, the next chapter takes us further into the technique of embodied role work, and how it too can be used within the one-to-one frame.

References

Casson, J. (2007). Psychodrama in Miniature. In C. Baim, J. Burmeister, M. Maciel (eds.), *Psychodrama Advances in Theory and Practice*. Routledge.

Daniel, S. (2007). Psychodrama, Role Theory and the Cultural Atom: New Developments in Role Theory. In C. Baim, J. Burmeister, M. Maciel (eds.), *Psychodrama Advances in Theory and Practice*. Routledge.

Frohn, E. and Klein, U. (2016). Morenos Soziales Atom in der psychodramatischen Tischinszenierung. *Zeitschrift für Psychodrama und Soziometrie*, 15(2), 313–326.

Holmes, P. (1992). *The Inner World Outside: Object Relations Theory and Psychodrama*. Routledge.

Homeyer, L. and Sweeney, D. (2016). *Sandtray Therapy*. Routledge.

Moreno, J.L. (1978). *Who Shall Survive?* (3rd ed.). Beacon House.

Turner, B. (2005). *The Handbook of Sandplay Therapy*. Temenos Press.

Van Gennep, A. (1961). *The Rites of Passage*. University of Chicago Press.

Winnicott, D. (1971). *Playing and Reality*. Tavistock.

Chapter 4

Working with role

Anna Chesner

The previous chapter gave a number of examples of how concretisation and work with miniatures brings a perspective on lived roles into the consulting room, whereby the concept of role as "a way of being" is crucial. In this chapter I consider role taking, a distinctive technique that involves:

a) the body in action;
b) an approach where the principle of "as if" is used to bring relationships from the client's interpersonal or intrapsychic world into the room;
c) an approach where there is a clear boundary between the here and now space of dialogue with the therapist, and the stage area where role relationships are explored in action.

Working with role as technique brings a heightened intensity into the room. The immediacy of engaging with an external person or part of self where there is a problematic or emotionally charged relationship is usually experienced by the client as a bigger therapeutic risk than working with concretisation. The therapist needs to be sensitive to this fact when suggesting the use of role, and mindful of the importance of warming up to the moment of role taking.

Stepping into the shoes of the other – role taking and interview in role

In this example the client, Brian, is working on his relationship with his new partner. They are happy together, but in this session he returns to a repeated refrain in his therapy: "Why does she get so upset with me?"

THERAPIST: I suggest we explore this question in a different way today. In a moment, I am going to invite you to move into the other chair over there, and to take on the body posture of Felicity. You are going to feel your way into her role, and I am going to ask "her" a few questions. If you need to say anything as yourself, Brian, please come back to your own chair and your own role. I'm only going to address you as Felicity in that chair, and you will respond as Felicity in the first person, with "I". Are you open to try this?

CLIENT BRIAN: Sure, I'll try, but this is something new for me.

THERAPIST: Well, it's an experiment, let's both approach it with an open mind. We will discuss the experience afterwards.

Commentary

There are a couple of important points about the setting up of this simple but powerful exercise. Firstly, the invitation to go into action is negotiated between therapist and client. The period of negotiation is part of the warm-up to the experience. It is framed as an experiment rather than a performance. Secondly, the rules of engagement are made clear. The client has the autonomy to return to his own role if he is unable to stay in role as his partner, and the therapist will ensure that he only speaks from the role of the other when in the chair designated for that role. This is a matter of psychological hygiene. It is essential that there is role clarity and that the distinctiveness of each person's experience in the relationship is respected. If he slips into "she" statements from the role of Felicity, he needs to be directed back promptly to his own chair and role. The therapist is also warming up to a different role within the session. Rather than being simply a partner in dialogue, as is normal within a more verbal reflective phase of the session, the therapist needs to access the internal role of psychodrama director. It is from within this more directive role that the therapist can best attend to the hygiene of the method.

THERAPIST: I'm just shifting this empty chair a little in preparation for the role of Felicity. (This small movement constitutes the creation of an area for action. Brian moves across to the empty chair and sits down.)

THERAPIST: Take your time, find your way of sitting as Felicity, your sense of what you are wearing, how you hold your body, your head, your breathing ... Hello, Felicity.

BRIAN AS FELICITY: Hello, who are you? (with a wry smile, marking the fact that he is mentalising himself and other; he knows we are in a different mode of being, that he is at one level still Brian, and at another level being true to the role of Felicity)

THERAPIST: I'm Brian's therapist, and we've brought you here today to help us understand what happens when you get upset with him. Maybe you can start by telling us how you met.

FELICITY: We met at work, we were colleagues at that point, and I was going through a divorce, and Brian was there for me. We used to go and get coffee together, and sometimes lunch. He was really kind, not like my ex ... we got really close, as friends, you know ... then one thing led to another and we've been together for nearly a year now and living together for three months.

THERAPIST: And how's that going, living together?

BRIAN AS FELICITY: Not great, well partly okay, but maybe it was too soon for me. He moved in with me, that's what we decided, but now … (with a lowering of the eyes)

THERAPIST: (after a moment) Go on, what are you in touch with?

BRIAN AS FELICITY: It feels like, now that we are living together, he expects me to be so much more robust than I feel. I don't like it when he's brusque with me, just over little things. I miss the Brian who used to take me for coffee. He was my knight in shining armour (Figure 4.1).

Commentary

The interview starts with some questions to help Brian get used to speaking as Felicity, and to tell their story as a couple from her point of view. Even though this story is familiar to both Brian and the therapist, telling it from her perspective is an important warm-up for Brian to begin to approach his question of what is upsetting her. To a greater or lesser extent, we all carry a sense of those we are in relationship with within us. The technique of role taking allows us to fully engage with that sense of the other, including, as we see in the short piece above, a sense of how the other sees and experiences us in the relationship.

> … Then I will look at you with your eyes
> And you will look at me with mine.
>
> Moreno (1915)

We re-join the session a few moments later.

THERAPIST: Thank you, Felicity. Brian, come back over to your own role. Brian, as you return to your own chair and your own role, let's leave Felicity here for a moment (indicating the now empty chair). Take a moment. What would you like to share?

BRIAN: Well, that was really interesting, much easier than I thought it would be. I could feel how she feels, and how she feels about me. I don't feel as irritated with her as I did when I came in. I think we have some things to talk about together. How we want to be with each other in this new phase of the relationship. What I didn't say in the role but was very much in touch with was the history of her relationship with her ex in that flat. It's like his shadow is still there in some way, for her, and maybe for me.

THERAPIST: (shifting the chair back to its neutral position in the room) Let's de-role the chair and continue our conversation.

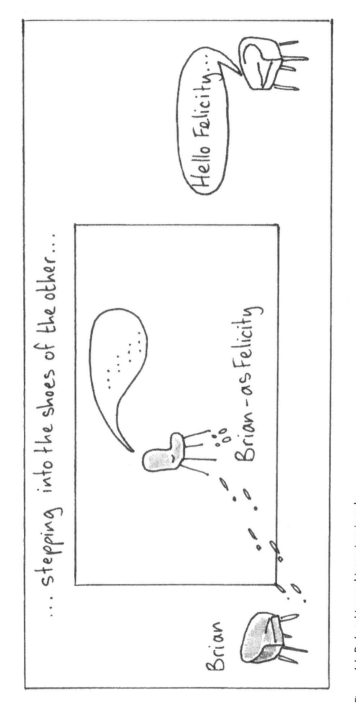

Figure 4.1 Role taking and interview in role

Commentary

The particular moment for de-roling is a matter of sensitivity on the part of the therapist. In this example it seems helpful to leave the chair "active" for a little while before de-roling it, to keep the sense of the other present for some moments in the room. It may be that the client wishes or needs to return to the role to explore something further. At a certain moment, a few minutes before the end of the session, it is advisable to completely de-role it in order to mark the return to the one-to-one relationship of client and therapist and to have some time where both are clearly in the dialogic here and now of the session, and not in the realm of "as if".

Role as encounter with the other

During the conversational part of a session, the key relationship in the room is between therapist and client. Relationships with other people are named and discussed in the third person. There is a massive difference in intensity between "I am angry with him" and "I am angry with you", between "I miss her" and "I miss you."

Even without taking on the role of the other, we can invite a powerful engagement with the role relationship by giving an "as if" space in the room to the other and facilitating an encounter with them. In this example, the client, Paul, a man in his late fifties, has been making a link between his current sexual difficulties and his early role relationship with his mother, a woman who both depended upon him emotionally at the time of her divorce, and who was verbally and physically abusive to him throughout his childhood.

THERAPIST: Paul, we have been exploring for some time now how confusing and how painful things were for you with your mother when you were young. As we've discussed previously, it may be helpful for you to "bring her here", so to speak, so that you have the chance to say some of the things you have said to me directly to her.

PAUL: Well, of course she's dead now and has been for some years, but even the idea of bringing her here makes my heart race.

THERAPIST: Yes, she is dead now, but is very much a part of your inner world, and apparently there are things you never got the chance to say to her. I'd like to give you the chance to do that today if you feel ready.

PAUL: Yes, I don't know what I'll say or how to do this, but I would like to try. It feels a bit disloyal, but I don't want to go to a place of guilt again. Let's do it!

THERAPIST: Well, I will guide you through step by step, and if it feels too much, you can always come back to your seat, take a break, or let me know if it is enough for today.

Your first task is to choose a chair for yourself in this encounter, and a chair for your mother. Position them in a way that feels helpful for you in terms of your saying what you need to say.

PAUL: (gets up, chooses two chairs and positions them carefully facing each other and very close together, then increases the distance between them) (to the therapist) I'll never manage to say anything if she's in my space. In fact, I think I need even more space! (moves one chair further away) That's her in that chair, and that's close enough.

Commentary

The exploration of appropriate distance, or "proxemics", is an important part of the work (Dayton, 2015). It is a warm- up to Paul's feelings when in the presence of the other, and a part of the warm- up to what he may need to say. At a level of felt experience, it brings the other into the room. It is important that he configures the role relationship spatially, taking into account distance and position in the room. It is preferable that he does this himself, rather than the therapist doing it for him. This is for a number of reasons. Only he knows at a feeling level what the right distance is, and in this case, because mother was intrusive and made assumptions about him, it is particularly important that he gets in touch with his own sense of agency, which will empower him in the challenging work ahead.

THERAPIST: So take your place as yourself, either sitting or standing, and when you are ready, begin to say what you need to say.

PAUL: (hesitates) (to the therapist) this is hard.

THERAPIST: (as Paul's double, directing the gaze towards the empty chair) "Mum, it's hard to do this, my heart is pounding, but I have some things I need to say to you …"

PAUL: Mum, it *is* hard to do this, and I feel a bit guilty, but I need to say to you that it wasn't okay how you were with me when dad left. There were so many things that weren't okay. It wasn't okay to make me "your little man" when you needed comfort, and it wasn't okay to call me "pathetic, and just like your father" when you were cross, and it wasn't okay to slap me when you were frustrated or unhappy. You made me feel responsible for you, useless, trapped … (Figure 4.2)

Commentary

In this example, we see the therapist taking on the function of a double, speaking as the client, to help him begin to find words for the encounter with mother. In group psychodrama psychotherapy, having a continuous double during a piece of work, moving alongside protagonists, experiencing each phase of the work with them, and from time to time speaking as the protagonist, is an

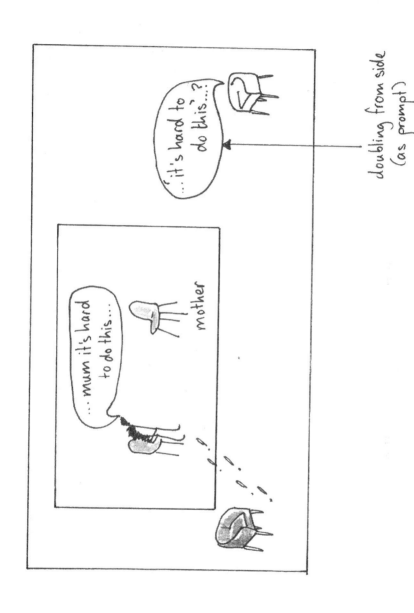

Figure 4.2 Paul's encounter with mother

immensely supportive function. An important role of the director/psychotherapist in a group setting is to check with the protagonist whether the double is right and give an opportunity for correction. Even a doubling statement that is off the mark can help the protagonist articulate their experience.

Within the one-to-one setting there are questions to be considered about how much the therapist doubles and whether this is done in the traditional position, physically alongside the client. The risk is that the client may feel that the therapist knows best and go along with what the therapist senses they "should" feel or say, rather than what is authentic. They may feel the therapist is being controlling and putting words into their mouth, which would be detrimental to the therapeutic alliance. On the other hand, it can be a lonely place to engage in role work, particularly when emotions are high and words are slow to come.

In the example with Paul, at the beginning of the encounter with mother the therapist offers a doubling statement as a prompt from the side. The words are fairly neutral, giving Paul a starting point for the encounter. The content comes from Paul, based on what he has already said in the session, and the therapist stays anchored in the here and now space of the consulting room within which the stage area of the encounter is contained and separate.

In some cases, it may be helpful for the therapist to come alongside the client for a while, taking on the role of double in the more conventional sense. If that is the choice, it is advisable to contract for this at the outset or at that moment in the work, to clarify that what is offered from the role of the double is an offer only, and that the client should either pick up and repeat in their own words what fits, or correct the statement. Therapists can usefully mark the moment they are moving from their regular position in their chair or standing at the side of the action, into the action area.

Let us return briefly to Paul's session.

PAUL: You made me feel responsible for you, useless, trapped … (flushes with emotion) and that's how I keep feeling in my relationship, I'm still not free …

THERAPIST: Let's give some space to these feelings here. Tell her!

PAUL: (standing) I need to do this standing. (breathing heavily, begins a growling sound which increases in volume) I don't have words, this is the sound of my anger from back then. It wasn't fair, and it wasn't right. I loved you, and you used me, abused me. (the catharsis of anger continues for a while until Paul indicates that it is enough and sits down, still facing the empty chair for the role of his mother, then turns to the therapist) I think that's it.

THERAPIST: I'm not going to invite you to reverse roles with your mother, as you have put yourself so much in her shoes already growing up. Let's stay with *your* experience here. When you are ready, de-role the two chairs and come back to your own chair.

Commentary

Working with the immediacy of role, it is not unusual for previously suppressed emotions to surface. In this example, space is given purely to the client's feelings of anger and outrage. It may be tempting to explore the internalised mother's response to Paul's outburst through the use of role reversal. In this case, it is reparative for Paul to stay with his own perspective and his own emotional truth, and for his anger to be validated and accepted by the therapist. In subsequent months, Paul will spontaneously access happier and more positive memories of his relationship with his mother.

The example shows how a two-part role relationship can be worked on without actually taking on the role of the other. It is worth remembering that the role relationship exists not only as a historical experience and narrative, but also as internal object relationship. The role relationship here can be described as that of a needy, manipulative, intrusive, abusive mother on the one hand and a compliant, confused, intruded upon child on the other. As an internalised role dynamic, the pattern reappears in the client's life in many emotionally close and intimate relationships, whereby he may find himself reliving either side of the role dynamic. So the significance of a felt change in his narrative about his historical relationship with his mother also signifies an internal shift that has the capacity to effect change in his present relationships.

Role and mirror, working with multiple perspectives

Psychodrama methods are intrinsically mentalisation-promoting (Napier & Chesner, 2014). The interplay and alternation of being in the reflective mirror position and being in role, whether as self or other, helps the client see and feel from multiple perspectives. This feature of psychodrama is evident in psychodrama as a group method, and with the help of some adaptations can be transferred to a good extent into the one-to-one setting.

To do this there needs to be a clear differentiation spatially between the area of the room used for action, and the area that will be used for reflection and witnessing. The boundary of these two spaces can be marked in a concrete way with a piece of cloth, ribbon or chairs.

The various roles within the system being explored (family, workplace, social) are each given a concretised space, perhaps a chair or a cushion, piece of cloth or sheet of paper marked with the name of the relevant role.

Because of the potential complexity of exploring multiple roles within a time-limited session, the therapist needs to be able to give clear directions around taking on a role, soliloquising from role, speaking as an aside, giving a message to another part of the system on the stage, reversing role or coming in to the mirror position to witness and reflect on what has been expressed onstage.

60 Anna Chesner

The therapist also needs a high level of emotional attunement to what is expressed physically and non-verbally, and whether these elements are aspects of the role being played or the client's response to the role.

As in the simpler examples of role work already given, the whole process should be transparently contracted for at the outset, and the rules of engagement made clear.

In the following example we meet Zara, a foreign student from Asia who has recently graduated from university and is struggling with what to do next with her life in the face of conflicting expectations and dreams.

CLIENT ZARA: They expect me to return home by the end of the summer, and I guess I should go, they do need me. But I can't face returning to my old life. I'm no way ready to leave my friends here, my girlfriend, my whole way of life. Do I go home, conform and live a lie, or do I come out to my family about who I really am and how I want to live my life?

THERAPIST: Would you like to take a look at the different expectations that you sense others have of you, and think about it together?

ZARA: Yes, it would be good to just unpack it, think about my options and the consequences of what I choose.

THERAPIST: Who are the relevant people for you?

ZARA: Mum, dad, grandma, my brother, my circle of friends here, my girl-friend …

THERAPIST: So firstly we need to define the action area and the audience space – that's where you and I can stand outside of the action and reflect on it together. Now start by marking a place for you within the action area. Use a cushion, a chair or cloth. That's you, then, there, in the action space. Now choose something to mark the place for each of the other people you have mentioned, and position them where you sense them in relation to you in the context of your current issue of what to do next with your life, and their expectations of you.

ZARA: (having now positioned various coloured cushions and a chair in the action space) Wow, I'm surrounded.

THERAPIST: Come into the audience and take a look from here.

ZARA: (moves to the side and takes a look at the image as a whole) Yes, that looks about right, and I am indeed surrounded! I can see it more clearly from here.

Commentary

Preparation for this kind of work is crucial. The definition of an action and audience area and the testing of it before the client goes into any roles serves as a safety net for role confusion or potential feelings of being over-whelmed. The therapist remains as far as possible in the audience or witness space, from where they can manage the action and keep the overview.

Working with role 61

By marking out the relevant roles in the action space, both client and therapist get a sense of the pace required to unpack and explore the different messages, and to leave enough time for de-roling and a post-action reflection phase of the work.

THERAPIST: When you are ready, I invite you to go and stand by each cushion/chair and feel your way into the role of that person. You can take on their physical posture and way of being. I will ask you to give your message from role to Zara. (indicating the chair for Zara in the action space) What do you expect from her, what do you think she should do? When you are ready, decide which role you want to begin with.

ZARA: Mother. (moving to the space designated for the mother role, then speaking as mother) But of course you will come home! Your room is waiting for you here, I know you have missed us, and we have missed you. Come home, we'll get a job for you in the family business, we will find you a nice boy. You will get married and live happily ever after. And I will be a grandmother! And your grandmother will be a great-grandmother. (sighs)

THERAPIST: Whose sigh is that – yours, mother, or Zara's?

ZARA: Zara's, mine.

THERAPIST: (attending to hygiene of role) Come into the audience space for a moment. (Zara moves to the side) You can either go into your own role here, resume that sigh and respond to her, or we can hear from all the relevant roles and then go into your role after.

ZARA: Let's hear all the messages first. Or I'll never get beyond dealing with mother!

THERAPIST: True! Who's next?

ZARA: Father! (moves to the relevant position) Just do as your mother says! She knows about these things. If you disappoint her, you will disappoint me. Don't disappoint me! (smiles in amused recognition)

THERAPIST: Come back to the audience space. Where next?

ZARA: Grandmother! (moves over to the chair and sits on it with her arms open towards Zara) Come home, darling! I am the matriarch of this family, and what I say goes. I know best how things should be. I love you very much, Zara, and I rely on you. The future of this family is in your hands. My life will be fulfilled when I see you married and with a family of your own. It is unthinkable that you would disappoint me in this. It is your duty! (moves out of role to the audience space, turns to the therapist) That's a killer!

THERAPIST: I see what you mean. Where next?

ZARA: Brother! (moves to his position) I am very busy with my own life, my friends, my future. I'm still at school, and in a couple of years I will also go away to study. I can't wait. The world is my oyster. I don't think I even notice what is happening for you. But secretly I'm glad the family pressure is on you rather than me. You take the heat, that suits me fine!

62   Anna Chesner

THERAPIST: Return to the audience space, and when you are ready, let's hear from the next role.

ZARA AS FRIENDSHIP GROUP: Don't go, you belong here now! Or go, and then come back. We understand you and accept you. We're all going our separate ways to some extent, but we're going to remain friends. The main thing is, be true to yourself. Don't make choices out of duty.

THERAPIST: Return to the audience space, and when you are ready, move into the remaining role.

Zara (moves to the closest cushion to her own role): I'm Bo, and I don't want you to leave. It hurts me that your family doesn't even know about me. They don't know I exist, let alone that you are in relationship with a woman. I don't know what will happen in our relationship, but right now neither of us want it to end. I know it's complicated for you, and I am not putting you under pressure, but … it's hard for me, too. (tearful)

THERAPIST: Are these tears yours, Bo, or Zara's?

ZARA AS BO: Both.

THERAPIST: Yes, it's a painful place to be. When you are ready, come back to the audience space. (Zara moves back to the side of the room)

ZARA: (to therapist) It is hard, I could feel each person's position and perspective.

THERAPIST: And now there is the opportunity to feel your own perspective, and the impact of their messages on you. When you are ready, go and stand in your own role and allow yourself to focus on the messages one by one. What do you want to say to them?

ZARA: (returning to the stage area, looking around at the various roles and spreading her arms out to her sides) This is how it feels, torn in two directions!

Zara then faces each of the designated roles one by one. Where necessary, the therapist prompts in the third person the key words Zara has spoken from the role of the others.

ZARA: (to mother) Yes, I know how you want my life to be. You've made it clear all my life. But I think you know it is wishful thinking, and I believe you understand me better than you let on.

THERAPIST: (prompting) And to father, who said "don't disappoint me, do as your mother says"?

ZARA: (to father) I don't want to disappoint you. But I'm a separate person from both of you. And I don't know how well you really know me. Maybe it's time you did get to know me better. (aside to therapist) That feels quite risky to say.

(to grandmother) This is so hard, you are not only my grandmother, you're my whole sense of tradition. I feel so guilty, I don't want to hurt you. I do take seriously my sense of duty, but ... right now I want to say to you – (aside to therapist) and I don't think I could say this in real life – that I also have a duty towards myself.

(to brother) You'll be fine whatever. I don't have an expectation of you. Maybe when you are older we can support each other more.

(to friendship circle) We are going to stay in touch, but what you don't or can't understand is just how different it is in my culture to be in a same sex relationship. It's easier here.

(to Bo) We will find a way. I feel torn between my feelings for you and my feelings for my family, and you know that. What's great is that you get it, you get how hard it is for me. I feel support from you. I don't want to lose you, or hurt you, but this is not simple for me.

THERAPIST: When you are ready, come to the audience space. Let's take a look at this whole scene together. What do you notice?

ZARA: (from mirror) What I see is a turning point in my life. When I was standing in there as me, I could feel each of these relationships separately, how they draw me in, or push me away. And the pull between home and here was really strong. I could feel it physically.

THERAPIST: What is your message to yourself, from the observing you in the audience space to the you that is "surrounded", as you say, with these conflicting pulls and expectations?

ZARA: (reflects) My message is: there is no easy solution to this. You have learned to be more independent and true to yourself by being over here these years. When you go back home, you need to take your independent thinker role with you. That doesn't mean you have to reveal everything about yourself to your family all at once. You can let them know you are thinking of working and living over here, that you don't necessarily want to work in the family business, that there are other options. The whole question of your sexuality, you don't have to throw that in their face all at once. That's a bigger question, and one that we need more time to think about.

At this point the space is de-roled and the rest of the session is used for reflection (Figure 4.3).

Commentary

The complexity of role relationships in this piece of work means that perspective changes and role changes need to be negotiated fairly succinctly. The directive to "give a message" helps to keep the work focused and to arrive at a felt "essence" of each role relationship. As with the use of concretisation, the position of observing ego, or mirror, mitigates against potential overwhelm. For Zara, it helps her change from an either-or formulation of her predicament to something more complex and differentiated. There is no attempt to rush to an easy solution of a complex problem. While the session itself

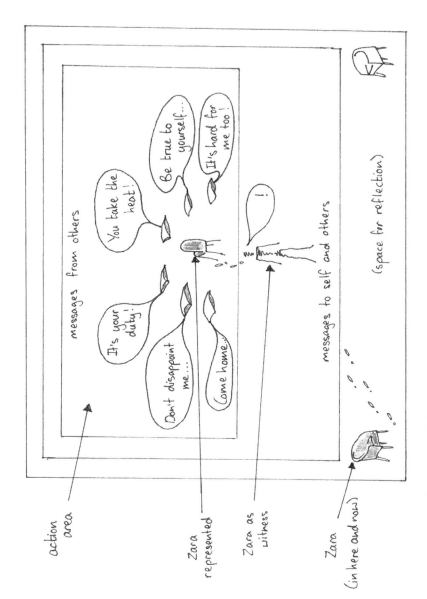

Figure 4.3 Role and mirror – working with multiple perspectives

Working with role 65

achieves a good level of closure, the questions articulated and explored are carried forward into future sessions.

Working with the double

When working with role, the technique of the double enables the client to explore the co-existence, perhaps discrepancy, between what can be expressed in a socially acceptable way and what might exist as an inner truth. Psychotherapy is a place that welcomes both authenticity and experimentation. Working with the technique of the double allows for the raw nature of what is felt to be expressed, while acknowledging that the consequences of such emotional honesty outside of the therapy frame could be inappropriate and even damaging for the relationship.

Let us return to Brian, whom we met above, role-reversing with his partner, Felicity. In this example, he begins to explore what he wants to say to her about the current state of their relationship. In the action area of the room he has placed two chairs, one for himself in the relationship and the other for Felicity. The chairs are facing each other in preparation for an encounter in the "as if".

THERAPIST: Begin in your own role. (Brian sits in his chair, facing Felicity)

BRIAN: I can see that you keep getting upset with me, and it hurts me to know that I am upsetting you. But I don't want to have to be on my best behaviour at home and always think about how you will react if I am anything other than sweetness and light. Something has to change.

THERAPIST: Come and stand behind your own chair and give a doubling statement, from that part of you that is *not* sweetness and light. Felicity won't be hearing this, but you will have a chance to get it off your chest.

BRIAN AS OWN DOUBLE: (moving to a position behind his chair) For fuck's sake, Felicity, stop making me feel guilty for everything that you feel, and like it's my job to make everything alright for you. I did that for years with my mother, and I've had enough of it for a lifetime. You're an adult, toughen up a bit! I'm not being mean to you, I just occasionally raise my voice or express some irritation about work, or something going wrong with my computer. You take it so personally. If I have to stifle all the little things, I'm going to erupt! No wonder our sex life isn't what it used to be. I'm so careful with you, I can't be spontaneous, and we're both losing out (Figure 4.4).

THERAPIST: How does that feel?

BRIAN: Great! Of course, I couldn't put it quite like that or she'll dissolve in tears and I'll be the bad guy again.

THERAPIST: Perhaps try it now, come back from doubling from behind the chair to sitting on it, as if really facing her, and see what feels right for you to say. (Brian sits back on the chair)

Figure 4.4 Working with the double

THERAPIST: Keep a sense of what you have just said as your own double, and also of Felicity in front of you and in relationship with you.

BRIAN: Felicity, I think I understand how it is for you when I lose my temper or raise my voice. I understand that you are still vulnerable or sensitive after your previous relationship and divorce, and maybe we need to talk about whether my moving in was too soon. I want you to understand something about me, too. I have spent so many years second guessing my mother's reaction to things, trying to make things alright for her, squashing down my own needs. I don't want to be in that role with you. I love you, and I want to be with you, but I need to be able to be me without fear of hurting you …

Commentary

As a method, the use of the double when encountering the other in role is particularly effective in fostering the expression of feelings and thoughts that are defended against or habitually suppressed. By giving a safe space for these thoughts and words to be spoken and heard, energy can be freed up for finding more moderate and appropriate language to prepare for an actual encounter with the other person.

Conclusion

As the examples above demonstrate, role taking, encountering in role and viewing the patterns of role relationships from multiple perspectives can be both powerful and containing. The techniques are used in intentional and explicit ways as punctuation within the dialogue of the therapy relationship. This is a less immersive approach than we find in group psychodrama psychotherapy, where protagonists fully enter the "as if" of scenes from their lives. Here, in the one-to-one setting, the continuous re-engagement with the reflective function/mirror position is paramount, so that there is an ongoing interplay between the experiential domain and the reflective one.

References

Dayton, T. (2015). *Neuropsychodrama in the Treatment of Relational Trauma.* Health Communications.

Moreno, J. L. (1915). *Einladung zu Einer Begegnung, Bericht von Jacob Levy.* Anzengruber Verlag Brüder Suschilzky.

Napier, A. & Chesner, A. (2014). Psychodrama and Mentalization: Loosening the Illusion of a Fixed Reality. In M. Farrall & K. Kirk (eds.) *Empowering Therapeutic Practice: Integrating Psychodrama into Other Therapies.* Jessica Kingsley.

Chapter 5

Working with addictions
The addictions compass and intergenerational action genogram

Anna Chesner

Psychodrama has a long history in the field of addictions. Zerka Moreno describes a powerful guest session she ran in a treatment programme in Italy. She placed an empty chair in front of a group of young addicts in a treatment centre in Italy, asking them to imagine a syringe of heroin on it, to get in touch with the message it sends them, and then to take the opportunity to respond to it (Moreno 2012, p. 441). Goldman and Morrison (1984) use numerous examples from their work with adult children of alcoholics, and Tian Dayton has published several works on her creative approaches to the addictions field (Dayton 1994, 2000, 2015).

Although not a specialist addictions therapist, I recognise that many issues which emerge in psychotherapy can usefully be looked at through an addictions lens. Most treatment centres favour group approaches to working with addictions, and psychodrama is frequently used in those settings. In this chapter I describe two psychodramatic approaches that I use where the perspective of addiction is relevant to the work.

The first of these is the addictions compass structure, which I originally developed as an exploratory tool within a psychotherapy group. That was a generic outpatient psychodrama psychotherapy group, but one where clients presented with a range of issues around alcohol, food and sex. I have subsequently fine-tuned the method, both for working in group as well as in the one-to-one setting.

The addictions compass structure

The structure allows the client to encounter their issue from several distinct perspectives, and to make affective and cognitive links between these. It can be used to explore both substance and behaviour-based addictive patterns. It requires the best part of a 50-minute session to set up, experience and reflect on.

Working with addictions   69

Preparation

The action area is prepared by the therapist to create a spatial container for the structured action. There is a central area, marked with a cushion or stool (preferably something without a back for full impact.) This area is for the role of the client (see Figure 5.1).

Facing and leading to this area from four different directions are four equal-sized cloths of different colours. The colours and textures can usefully be chosen to evoke the quality of the perspective to be taken from each position.

Before going into action, the particular addiction or addictive behaviour to be investigated is negotiated between client and therapist. Where there are multiple possibilities, choosing just one helps the work be specific, rather than generalised into a concept of "having an addictive personality".

The action

The client is introduced to the central cushion as the place that represents themself. They are then directed to hold four different roles and to give a message to "themself" on the central cushion.

From the first position (we can call this North) the client takes the role of the addictive substance or behaviour specifically in terms of what it *promises*. The therapist can prompt the role once the client is standing in the appropriate place:

THERAPIST: I am alcohol/cocaine/sex ... and I promise you ...

The client picks up the prompt and has the opportunity to name all the promises that the addiction makes. They are a kind of salesperson for the addiction. Some typical comments that arise from this role:

CLIENT: I promise you a rush/distraction/numbness/something to do when you are bored ... I promise to make you feel really good! Use me, you can rely on me, you know it makes sense. I promise I'm here for you!

Taking on the role of the addictive behaviour or substance can initially be experienced as quite fun. There may be an element of caricature, so that even while identifying with the role in its powerful and seductive aspect, there is the beginning of a more critical perspective on it. When the list of promises is exhausted, the therapist guides the action into the next place.

THERAPIST: Now move around clockwise (we could call this East). From this perspective, remain in the role of the substance or behaviour and carry on selling yourself to X, but this time more specifically in terms of what you *protect* X from. Tell her! "I protect you from ..."

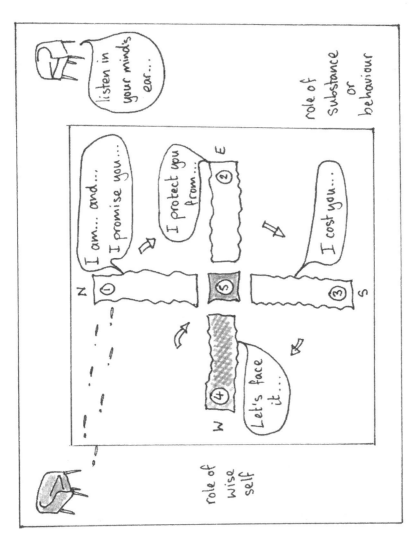

Figure 5.1 The addictions compass

Some typical comments that arise from this role are:

CLIENT: I protect you from your loneliness, your shyness, your feelings, getting overwhelmed, your memories, from having to face your trauma history, your shame, your inadequacy, your regrets. I protect you from engaging with life.

In this role, the client in role remains psychologically in allegiance with the addiction, continuing to sell it as having a useful function. At the same time, by naming what it claims to "protect" the client from, they are actually getting in touch with what they are *defending* against through the addiction. These are the experiences they will need to confront at some point in terms of therapeutic working through. It is important to engage with these brief moments of taking on the role of the substance or behaviour without judgement. The therapist positions themself as a companion at each stage of the exploration, without a sense of "should" or "shouldn't". A more judgmental stance would be likely to bring up resistance in the client. Instead, the defensive aspect of the addiction is acknowledged as at least offering an *apparent* benefit.

When the statements from this perspective are exhausted, the therapist moves the client around to the next space.

THERAPIST: Now move around clockwise (we could call this position South; the client is now standing directly opposite the space of promise) From this position, remain in role as the addiction, but this time get in touch with the perspective of the cost. Remind X what you cost her, what you have cost her, and what you may cost her. "I cost you …"

Typical responses from this role are:

CLIENT: I cost you … lots of money, your health, your figure, your relationship, your children, your fertility, your job, your dignity, your self-respect … I may cost you your life.

This perspective is often experienced as painful, moving and a place of sobering up. The reality is that addictions do take their toll and we pay a more or less heavy price for them. There is a significant difference in impact between an external person pointing this out, which many addicts have experienced repeatedly, and the addiction itself naming its price. Addiction is a Mephisthophelean pact.

In the first three roles, the client is exploring the role of the addiction, whether substance or addictive behaviour, each time with a slightly different focus. As they move to the fourth space, they need to move for the first time in this exercise into a role that is not the addiction, but an aspect of self.

THERAPIST: Now move round to the final space (we could call this West, and the client is directly opposite the aspect of the addiction that defends or claims to protect).

THERAPIST: You are now moving out of the role of the addiction, and into the role of your wise self. Perhaps you are comfortable with the term "higher self", or the part of you that can observe and reflect, make links, the part of you that knows – perhaps the part of you that chooses to come to therapy.

It is helpful to offer different words to warm the client up to this role. Some people have a negative or cynical response to the term "higher self" which is a central part of twelve- step programmes.

THERAPIST: From this position, get in touch with what you know, and tell X here what all this has to do with his/her history, and particularly with his/her relationship history.

Typically, responses from this role relate to early attachment issues and traumatic events in the client's life that have disrupted their development and led to avoidant behaviours in terms of intimate relationships.

CLIENT: You know what was going on in your life when you first turned to this addiction. You were overwhelmed by the impact of the family/relationship/issues around you/the trauma you were experiencing and witnessing. At that time, it seemed to be the only solution, but let's face it, you isolated yourself, you built a relationship with the addiction, and in some ways, you are still stuck at that place developmentally. You haven't learned how to be with others in a more open and healthy way. And you tell yourself it's okay, but you and I both know that it is not okay. It hurts, and it reduces your life ...

The details vary, but in essence this role stands for an aspect of the client that is pro-health, pro-social and pro-change. It seems that going through the three earlier positions of this exercise achieves a climax at this point. Some clients may need the therapist to double the statements from this role, to help the client warm up to it and for the role to find its language. It is important to be vigilant and notice if statements slip into the perspective of one of the other roles – for example, the Promise. It is vital for the therapist to point this out and keep the different roles hygienic and distinct.

Having been all around the external part of the compass, the final part of the exploration involves inviting the client to position themselves in the middle, on the cushion that represents themself as a whole. I often refer to this as "X central". The client is directed to remain in this place, and in the mind's ear (perhaps prompted by the therapist repeating some key phrases), to listen to the message from the Promise, the Protection, the Cost and the Wise Self roles. At each point, they may have a response, especially towards the message of the Wise Self, in a way that confirms and embeds that message for the client.

For the final part of the session, the physical structure of the compass is de-roled, and the client and therapist spend a few minutes reflecting on the experience. This may happen in a spontaneous way, or the therapist can guide the client through role feedback from each of the roles/positions, and a sharing process about the impact of the structure as a whole. In my experience, the reflective processing of this ritual structure can extend over a few sessions.

Intergenerational addictions action genogram

The addictions compass offers an exploratory method of engaging with the individual's experience of addiction and their personal relationship with it. The intergenerational addictions genogram provides a different perspective on the issue of addiction.

Transgenerational psychodrama, used particularly in group settings, was developed by Anne Ancelin Schützenberger, drawing on her systemic, group analytic and psychodrama psychotherapy trainings. Her explorations of the impact of trauma and family secrets through the generations can be read about in *The Ancestor Syndrome* (Schützenberger 1998)

The method described here draws on Schützenberger's work. It can be approached as an adaptation of the small world technique, using both concretisation and role (as described in Chapter 3) or can be seen in terms of role work, to look at intergenerational patterns of the family through the lens of addictions and trauma. The theme of trauma is included here alongside addictions as addictive behaviours frequently arise as attempted solutions to traumatic experiences and existential or developmental challenges. In the addictions compass, the aspect of trauma tends to come to light through the role of the Wise Self. In the intergenerational addictions genogram, the therapist enquires methodically about traumatic events and the responses to these through the roles of various family members across three or more generations. Where different family members are connected by a similar addictive or psychological response to life's challenges, these are marked by placing a coloured thread or ribbon between different members of the family system (see Figure 5.2).

The scale of this method can be adapted, depending on the size of the work space. In a smaller space the whole method can be done on a communicube or other small world stage, using the finger on the object to designate speaking from role. In a generously sized studio space the client can use chairs to

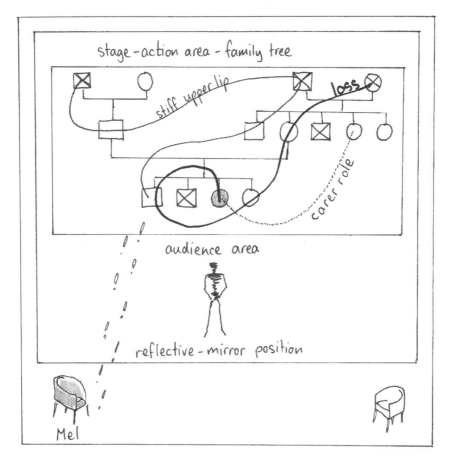

Figure 5.2 Intergenerational addictions action genogram

represent each role, and sit on these or stand behind them to embody the role. Alternatively, where there is sufficient space to move around, but not enough for the use of multiple chairs, roles are marked with cushions or pieces of card, and are embodied briefly in a standing position. Quite apart from the issue of available space, the therapist might choose small world as a means of bringing more aesthetic distance into the work, or cushions/chairs as a means of allowing more impact from each embodiment of the role.

I illustrate the method here with a fictional client, Mel, a 30-year old woman who binge drinks and uses recreational drugs – behaviours that are beginning to affect her physical health, mental well-being and her capacity to perform her job as a junior doctor.

THERAPIST: Let's explore the theme of addictive behaviours across the generations of your family. Mark your own role with a cushion and place a cushion for each of your siblings alongside you, in a line and in the sequence of your age.

MEL: Well, I'm the middle of three, so here is my brother Andy, who is five years older than me, and here is my sister Fey, who is two years younger.

THERAPIST: Okay, now, a little behind the generation of yourself and your siblings, place a cushion for your father on the left, as we look at this, and one for your mother on the right. Place further cushions for each of their siblings, alongside them and in the order of their birth.

MEL: Dad is an only child, and mum has three siblings. Actually, she had four, but one died in childhood.

THERAPIST: Let's include all the siblings, including the one who died.

MEL: Now I think about it, my mother lost a baby too, between my brother and me, a late miscarriage.

THERAPIST: Let's mark that lost baby too, with a cushion in the appropriate place. We'll come back to the significance of this shortly.

Finally let's go back a generation to your grandparents and mark them, the paternal grandparents just behind your father, and the maternal grandparents behind your mother and your maternal aunts and uncles. Finally, if there is anyone else, who you think might be relevant to this theme mark their place with a cushion. We may not have time for all your cousins, for example, but if there are one or two of them, or the spouses of your maternal aunts and uncles who seem relevant here, let's put them in.

Having marked out three generations, there are fourteen cushions in the space. Since this exploration is being done within a 50-minute session frame, the therapist needs to manage time accordingly, which is done by asking specific questions to the client, who inhabits the role of each part of the system briefly.

THERAPIST: Starting from Andy, make a statement about what life has presented you with, and what behaviours you use to manage this. What is your message to Mel about life?

MEL AS ANDY: (standing by the cushion marking his role) I am really successful in my career, I don't have a problem. I work a lot to look after my own family ... actually, I probably work too much! My message is, immerse yourself in work, be successful, earn money!

MEL AS LOST BABY: I was never born, but I left a legacy and a lot of pain and fear in the family. My message to Mel is, life is full of pain and loss, but also, life goes on.

MEL: (as an aside to therapist) I can feel now how that loss prior to my birth has been around at a feeling level all my life. I'm the one who wants to make it all alright, I work hard as a doctor, but can't be at peace.

MEL AS FEY: I'm the angry one in the family, and the wild child. I do quite a lot of drugs, socially. My message to Mel is, life is too short to be taken seriously. Have fun, don't think too much!

THERAPIST: Now move back a generation and let's hear the messages from your parents' generation.

MEL AS FATHER: Life is about responsibilities. I work hard, have always worked hard. I show my love in practical ways. There's no point wallowing in emotion. A nice single malt or two at the end of the day and some peace and quiet. That's my recipe for a good life.

MEL AS MOTHER: (tearfully) I was very close to my little brother, who died when I was small. Life has presented me with losses that I haven't been able to process. I don't talk about feelings. I just get on with things, cooking, housework … but carry a cloud of unspoken sadness around with me.

MEL AS UNCLE: It was hard for me when our little brother died, and I was old enough to understand what was going on. I was always the eldest son, and then the only son. I like to eat, and am quite obese if truth be told. My message to Mel is, eat your feelings, it works for me!

MEL AS AUNT: I feel a real closeness with Mel. I was a replacement child, too! I also work in the health professions, as a nurse. I've always felt not good enough, and my solution has been to devote myself to work. My message is, whatever you do isn't enough, do more!

THERAPIST: Let's hear the message from your uncle who died in childhood.

MEL AS DECEASED UNCLE: I died of meningitis, I think, at age four. I left a hole in the family, I know that. My message is that unexpected and terrible things happen that are unbearable, too much. Life is too much!

THERAPIST: And now let's move back a generation to the four grandparents, what life presented them with, and how they responded.

MEL AS PATERNAL GRANDFATHER: Mel never knew me, as I died relatively young. I was a pilot in the Second World War, never spoke about it, lucky to survive. My message to the family is maintain the stiff upper lip, it won us the war!

MEL AS PATERNAL GRANDMOTHER: I'm still alive, I have dementia. I was a housewife most of my life, used to be a dab hand at bridge! My message is get on with things, be practical, don't ask too many questions. "Least said, soonest mended!"

MEL AS MATERNAL GRANDFATHER: I grew up during the war, I was too young to fight, but my own father died in it when I was very young, so I never knew him. It was a struggle for my mother. My message: life is a struggle. My solution: I spent a lot of time at the pub!

MEL AS MATERNAL GRANDMOTHER: I suffered from depression quite a lot in my later years. I died shortly after my husband did. I'd been taking a lot of

Working with addictions   **77**

antidepressants and sleeping pills over the years. I don't think I ever got over losing my child. My message ... life is hard, too hard.

Commentary

Having marked out key roles in the family over three generations and having heard through brief role reversal what life presented to Mel's family members and how they responded to life's challenges, it is now time for her to take a look at any patterns that are becoming apparent, and to concretise these patterns. The psychodramatic perspective here is that of the mirror, the space from which there can be an overview.

THERAPIST: Thank you, Mel, now come out into mirror, where you can see the bigger picture, with me. As you look at the different personalities, their responses to life's challenges, and their implicit messages to you, let's think together about any themes that we see going through the generations.

MEL: The first theme I see is loss. There's my mother's loss of her brother, and then her own late miscarriage.

THERAPIST: Can you mark this theme with a ribbon passing through the generations?

Mel places a black ribbon between her maternal grandmother, her mother and herself, looping it to include her two siblings.

MEL: The other theme I see is to do with the stiff upper lip, which I think links with using alcohol or other substances.

She places a red ribbon from her paternal grandfather to her father and down to her brother, and then revises it to include her maternal grandfather and uncle.

MEL: What I see here is that these themes are connected. There is pain and loss in life, but as a family we seem to try all sorts of ways of not facing it, we overwork, overeat, overdrink, use drugs, whether pharmaceutical or recreational ... it's sobering! I'm struck by the link between my aunt and myself, we are both girls who follow the death of a brother and both go into the health professions. I'd like to place this yellow ribbon between my aunt and me. I also notice that it's the male line that seems to hold the message of keeping a stiff upper lip, but the women join in, like it's something that can't be questioned.

THERAPIST: That seems like a good place to pause. Take a final look at the image, the roles involved, and the coloured threads through the generations. When you are ready, de-role the action space.

78 Anna Chesner

Mel de-roles the materials and the cushions and returns to the dialogue space with the therapist.

THERAPIST: Let's take a few minutes to reflect on how this was, and anything that we want to mark as material to return to …

Commentary

This method enables both the therapist and client to see intergenerational connections in a concrete way. The visual and kinaesthetic impact of the client marking these connections between the generations with a coloured ribbon or cloth is considerable. The intervention brings the benefit of helping the client to acknowledge the bigger picture. This includes cultural norms (such as the stiff upper lip), historical factors (the Second World War), existential factors (the loss of a child or sibling) and systemic factors (the lack of emotional working through on the part of the grandparental and parental generations presenting a problem to the children). In terms of role analysis, life presents us with various challenges, and the behavioural response to these challenges is driven by beliefs, which are usually implicitly rather than explicitly held within the family system. In Mel's case, there is a belief in her family that trauma cannot or should not be spoken about, and that it is better to get on with the doing of life, rather than spend time mourning or expressing feelings together. This attempted solution to life's challenges brings side effects and consequences with it as addictive behaviours are used to deflect from the unexpressed and unacknowledged pain. The material that emerges in this action structure is dense, and as with the addictions compass, may take several sessions to process, and will inform future conversations as the therapy process continues over time.

While it is important for each individual in therapy, whether group or one-to-one, to take responsibility for their own response to life's challenges, it is vital to recognise such behaviours and patterns as having a systemic and intergenerational meaning. When we explicitly come to understand our own way of being as something that is informed by our family and cultural narratives, we can begin to question the implicit beliefs that drive our actions – an important step towards contemplating change.

References

Dayton, T. (1994). *The Drama Within: Psychodrama and Experiential Therapy.* Health Communications.

Dayton, T. (2000). *Trauma and Addiction: Ending the Cycle of Pain through Emotional Literacy.* Health Communications.

Dayton, T. (2015). *Neuropsychodrama in the Treatment of Relational Trauma*. Health Communications.

Goldman, E. E. & Morrison, D. S. (1984). *Psychodrama: Experience and Process*. Kendall/ Hunt.

Moreno, Z. (2012). *To Dream Again*. Mental Health Resources.

Schützenberger, A. (1998). *The Ancestor Syndrome: Transgenerational Psychotherapy and the Hidden Links in the Family Tree*. Routledge.

Chapter 6

Psychodramatic dream work

Anna Chesner

Not all clients bring dreams to psychotherapy, and some only bring dreams occasionally, but for others the exploration of their dream world is a central feature of their therapeutic journey.

Dreams have characteristics that evoke dramatic or filmic reality. They are characteristically scenic, one episode moving to another in quite expressionistic and surprising ways. There is often an awareness in the dreamer of a point of view, a spectator viewpoint and an actor viewpoint – a sense of close perspective or distance. They are potent with "surplus reality", the term Moreno (1966) used to describe imagination-based phenomena, events that might never happen in real life, but which are charged with *added* reality, rather than diminished for that fact. In other words, dreams, like drama, transcend the limitations of everyday reality, while speaking to the dreamer's innermost sense of self in their internal and external world.

Dreams are intrinsically creative, the product of unconscious mental activity that attempts to make sense of the many external factors of everyday life as well as the multiplicity of internal impulses, sensations and preoccupations of the inner world of the client. They use the language of imagery to communicate with the dreamer. By sharing these images and sequences of images with the therapist as "interested other", clients focus their own curiosity on the dream material and on their own conscious resonances and associations with that material. The therapist's own perspective adds a further dimension to the exploration of potential meaning. Whether the dream is discussed verbally or worked with in action, there is something about the shared curiosity that invites further layers of meaning to be revealed.

In classical psychodrama as a group psychotherapy, there is a known form for dream exploration that is immersive and very powerful, and needs to be acknowledged before considering appropriate techniques in the one-to-one setting. Written about by Grete Leutz (1986), it involves a number of stages. The protagonist enacts their preparation for going to bed, and their falling asleep prior to the dream that is to be explored. This locates the dream as an event in time, and helps the protagonist get in touch with whatever preoccupations and emotions may have been around for them leading up to the dream event – in other words, the context of the dream. As they lie down to sleep on the "as if" of the stage bed, they are given a few moments to dream the dream in their mind's eye, usually with the lights dimmed to aid the process. The stage "bed" is then moved to the side and the dreamer stands and enters the dream world, thus showing it to the group on the psychodramatic stage. Role reversal is used to unpack the dynamic of the action and the relationships. Everything that is dreamt is explored through role reversal, whether an atmosphere, a colour, a disembodied voice, an animal, person or object. In the process meaning emerges, not through direct interpretation, but as a consequence of shining the light of attention on the various roles, role relationships and themes of the dream material. When the dream has been explored to the point at which the dream actually ended, the dreamer is given the opportunity to "dream the dream on" in action. This means stepping into a further level of surplus reality and choosing an additional scene or interaction on the dream stage as a way of bringing resolution or completion.

Finally, the dreamer/protagonist returns to the bed scene where they started, closes their eyes and is directed to "dream the dream again", quietly in their mind's eye, in its new version with the additional scene or action where appropriate. When they are ready, they "awake" and there may follow a role training scene, in which the wisdom of the dream is taken into action, perhaps by initiating a much-needed conversation with a loved one, or maybe by giving themself a new message as they embark on a new day in a new way.

Within the one-to-one frame there are numerous approaches to working with dreams. With the shorter session time and the lack of auxiliaries to hold roles, the conventional classical group psychodrama structure needs to be substantially adapted, and this can be done flexibly, according to the creative impulse of both client and therapist. Just as dreams pay no attention to the Aristotelian unities of time, place and action, the psychodrama psychotherapist and client can also play with scale and multiple techniques within the one session and the one dream exploration. The anchor for this exploration is the dialogic relationship from the position of the two chairs of psychotherapist and client in the here and now of the therapy session.

The exploration usually begins with a simple narration of the dream, which may be done either in the past tense, as an unpacking of the memory of the dream, or in the present tense, which brings more immediacy. Note the difference between "I was in a building, somewhere upstairs …" and "I am in a building, somewhere upstairs …".

Any use of action techniques is preceded and followed by here and now reflection. While this is true of all one-to-one psychodrama sessions, it is worth noting particularly at this point because there is something hypnotic about entering or recreating the dream world, and we do need to make sure that the client is well grounded in the here and now as they leave the

82 Anna Chesner

session after such an exploration. There follow some vignettes of dreams explored in action with reflections on the value of the techniques used.

Scene setting and use of role

Max, a young man in his late twenties who came to therapy initially to work on his difficulty in maintaining intimate relationships, brings a dream in which he finds himself hiding in the corner of a ship's cabin, looking towards the door and watching as water floods in. It is part of a series of dreams involving water from which he usually wakes up frightened.

He is asked how he would like to explore the dream, and he replies that he would like to recreate just that one moment from the dream in the therapy room. Although the dream was frightening, he has a sense that he needs the physical experience of his posture and the setting of the scene to begin to make sense of it.

THERAPIST: Let's decide on how we will configure the room so that you have a clear stage area, and so that you can step back out of the dream into our space here at any point if it becomes too intense – a place of "dry land".

Max sets up the stage space, marking the key features of the dream setting, walls, wardrobe, porthole and water with cloths. He then positions himself in the corner of the room, onstage. He turns half towards the wall, with his arms cupping his head, and looks towards the cloth representing the water pouring into the cabin.

MAX: That's it, that's how it is.

THERAPIST: So take a moment, hold that posture, and speak from role from within the dream cabin ... what are you in touch with as you stand in that corner with the water flooding in?

MAX: I'm hiding, but I'm trapped. I feel contained by the walls, by my arms, I'm breathing fast and I can feel my heart beat ... I'm wondering what to do, I could drown here, but there's nowhere to go ... I need to get out of here!

THERAPIST: Step out of role and leave the stage area for a moment. When you are ready, come into the role of the water and find your physicality in the role.

Max steps onto the cloth representing the water flowing into the cabin and gestures with his arms and whole body towards the corner where Max is hiding.

MAX: I'm the water, I come from outside and I am flowing in, nothing can hold me back, I am a force of nature, endless, life-giving, life-taking. It's not personal, I just am ...

Psychodramatic dream work   83

Commentary

Through a simple role reversal, Max is able to experience both sides of the role dynamic the dream presents him with. He is both the water and the one threatened by it. We can think about this dream in terms of role analysis, exploring the five factors of context, behaviour, feelings, assumptive beliefs and consequences. In role analytic terms, he finds himself faced with a force that is greater than him, that is to do with life itself. This is the context of role: what he is faced with. His response is to try to hide and to seek the comfort of something solid by turning away from life. This is the behavioural response within the dream. His feelings are predominantly fear, with an element of loneliness. While he wants to escape, he experiences himself within the dream as trapped, in danger of drowning, and helpless. These beliefs are immediately clear from the action of the dream. The fact of his being alone in the ship's cabin points also to a belief in his fundamental aloneness at this time in facing life's challenges. The consequence of this and similar dreams is that he wakes up alarmed, and becomes aware that there is something going on for him that he needs to explore or change.

The purpose of the exploration in action is to get in touch with the felt experience of the dream. The task for the therapist here is to determine how much enactment is enough, and how much time to give to reflecting together on the experience.

THERAPIST: Okay, Max, when you are ready, de-role the scene and come back to the here and now of the therapy space.

How was the experience?

MAX: It was scary, but it was different because you were here. It made it more bearable, and that makes me think. I do feel very alone in facing life's challenges at the moment. We've been speaking about that here quite a lot. I try to set up structures for myself, to be in control. I've always tried to be strong and present myself as coping, but it is all a bit overwhelming. I do have people in my life, but when it comes to the big challenges, I always feel like I'm on my own. Thinking about the dream, maybe putting myself in a corner isn't the best response. I know it's a cliché, but maybe I need to learn to go with the flow!

Commentary

The exploration of this one dream moment in action feeds into a dialogue that helps to contextualise the dream as part of an ongoing therapeutic process relating to life themes and Max's overdeveloped and underdeveloped roles in response to life's challenges. The role reversal with water is particularly significant for Max. By being in role as the symbol of what he

84 Anna Chesner

initially experiences as threatening, he is able to get in touch with and to some extent embody and own the transpersonal quality of the flow of life. This in turn changes his perspective on himself, and particularly on his overdeveloped role of the independent one who needs to be in control.

Communicube and small world

The use of small world concretisation allows a dream to be looked at together by client and therapist, scene by scene. The focus shifts freely from the representation of the dream to the reflective dialogue, and back.

Here we meet Regina, who brings the first of many dreams that punctuate her therapy. This is in the third session. I begin with an account of the dream content.

The dream

Scene 1: A male work colleague is asking Regina and two others to spoon some stuff into three pots. She is in a nightie, and is aware that she is wearing inappropriate clothing.

Scene 2: She goes out and is in an old house, which then turns into an estate. An old woman is standing at the front door and tells Regina not to go down that path, as there is a man there and she is not appropriately dressed.

Scene 3: She is a little girl, on an ice or glass staircase, alone, and looking down.

Scene 4: She finds herself on another level. A female friend from years ago is there, someone who has since died. She is part of a team of women, and her message to Regina is "You're not part of this, you can't be here".

The communicube is used to display each of the scenes (Casson 2007). Regina chooses small objects to map out the image and to unpack any resonances that come up from what she sees. We begin at the top level of the communicube, where she represents the three colleagues and herself, and the three pots. In her reflections, she shares about the sense of belonging that she had had in that team of work colleagues, a few years ago. She notes that this was a contrast to her early experience at home, where she was very much the outsider as the very much younger third of three siblings. Considering the fact that she is wearing a nightie amongst former work colleagues, she remembers situations at home as a child where she was in her nightie and trying to cover herself fully in front of the others in an environment characterised by emotional neglect and verbal and physical abuse.

The second scene is placed on the next level down on the communicube. A figure is chosen to represent the old woman at the threshold, and a ring of fire to represent the warning not to go that way. She chooses not to represent the man who is the reason for the warning.

She reflects on the scene and discloses how as a child on the estate where they moved to, there were older boys who behaved inappropriately with her, and how, in retrospect, she was without protection, guidance or even a voice at that time.

This disclosure leads into the central third scene, where she is sitting at the top of a glass or ice stairway looking down. For this scene, Regina clears the communicube and places the figure of a sitting fairy at the top level. She is moved to see the solitude and vulnerability of the little girl, sitting precariously at the top of the stairs in a place of transparency, exposure and coldness.

REGINA: That's just how I used to sit, that looks like me at about age three. She's all alone, it's so bleak.

THERAPIST: What's your message to her today, from your adult self, witnessing her, in the dream, and in the therapy room?

REGINA (TEARFULLY): I'm here with you … and will sit alongside you!

Commentary

At this point the technique of concretisation is augmented through a role encounter with self. This is an emotionally intense moment. At one level, it is a reparative message: what was missing in the past in terms of care, protection and attunement is offered in the present, from the adult to the frightened child. At another level, the message is an encouragement from self to face the therapy journey which is just starting, and possibly also a direction to the therapist – "I need you to sit alongside me."

Returning to the communicube, the final scene is concretised: another group of three people is set up, and the message "You're not part of this, you can't be here" is spoken. The words are repeated, to let their impact sink in.

The scene sits in contrast to the opening scene of the dream, where she had recognised herself as having belonged to a group of colleagues. The memories evoked by the final scene of the dream are more ambivalent. The friend who speaks the significant words in the dream is remembered as someone Regina was close to, but on further discussion it emerges that she also used to habitually exclude her in their shared friendship group. The experience of not being part of things has been pervasive in her life, but not all-pervasive.

After de-roling the communicube, there is time for reflection on the dream as a whole. Key themes that the dream exploration has brought into the therapy space are:

belonging and not belonging (amongst colleagues, old friends, and in the family of origin);

exposure and vulnerability (wearing inappropriate clothes, being unprotected and alone);

archetypal elements (the fairy tale elements of the three pots, the old woman giving a warning at the threshold of her journey, the glass stairway).

Each of the themes identified in this dream run through the ensuing therapy, and some dream elements recur in later dreams. At an emotional level within the session, the most significant moment was the encounter between the lone vulnerable child within the dream and the supportive adult role in the therapy space, facilitated and witnessed by the therapist. This presages some deep work on Regina's relationship with her mother, as well as her own relationship as a mother with her daughter. Her mother's repeated refrain to her as a child, "You know I never wanted you, love …", was a deeply rejecting message, but one that was delivered in a paradoxically affectionate way. This locus formed the foundation of her ongoing issues with belonging and not having a right or a place in the world.

Drawing and role approach to dream work

Art media can also be used to depict dreams, either for direct discussion in the session, or as a first step towards working with role or concretisation. I always have large pads of cartridge paper and a variety of pastels and wax crayons to hand so that these can be accessed easily. Regina had a recurrent image that occurred both in sleep and as a waking dream as a felt sense, a lived metaphor. Indeed, it was this repeated experience that prompted her to engage with therapy in the first place. The image was of being alone in a small boat, adrift on a vast expanse of water, in a place where there is no distinction between the water and the mist that surrounds it. There is no wind, no waves, no horizon: the doldrums.

The drawing pad becomes the frame for this piece of action work. It has a natural and obvious boundary, within which the power of the imagination allows the client to bring to life the sense of the image. In Regina's case, she chooses the largest available pad and sits on the floor. She chooses a grey pastel, which she lightly and repeatedly brushes across the paper. The image is indistinct, and the act of slowly building up the mist is immersive. Gradually, in the middle of the page, a very small and indistinct boat appears, and what appears to be the shape of a figure bent forward. At the edge of the page and reaching to the full height of the page is the edge of what might be a large tree.

Regina returns to her chair and looks at the image, which she begins to describe.

REGINA: You see how small the boat is, and the little figure hunched over in it, that's how it feels, being adrift in the vastness of the water with no reference point. I'm really alone, lost and helpless. The boat is a little container, a kind of protection, like my posture, curled over. But the very thing I do to protect myself in my aloneness keeps me where I am. It's self-perpetuating. And I have felt like that even in the midst of friends.

THERAPIST: And what's this at the edge of the page – a tree?

REGINA: It's an Ent, like in *Lord of the Rings*. They're wise and ancient. It's also me, the one who is witnessing, dreaming. There's such a massive distance between this me and the one in the boat. She seems unreachable.

Commentary

There is something interesting happening at this moment, in terms both of scale and of role. From the perspective of scale, there is a vastness represented within the confines of a relatively small frame, the page. Within that image itself there are two Reginas: the small one, almost foetal, lost, adrift and alone, and the observing one, witnessing, but unable to reach the boat. Outside of the image is the here and now dimension of the therapy space, in which both therapist and client are witnesses to the inner drama depicted on the page, clearly much larger than either of the two Reginas on the page. The apparent impossibility of contact within the dream image is paradoxically contradicted by the act of sharing and co-reflection in the therapy room.

THERAPIST: Would you be interested in giving voice to the different roles within your dream?

Place your finger on the figure in the boat. What is she saying?

REGINA AS THE FIGURE IN THE BOAT: (quietly) Find me, I am all alone and frightened. I can't do this on my own ...

THERAPIST: And now place your finger on the figure at the side of the page. What does she say?

REGINA AS WATCHER: I see you, I see how far adrift you are, and I want to reach you ...

THERAPIST: And finally, from your own place in the here and now, looking at these roles in the dream?

REGINA: A memory is coming up. I am remembering being very young, I'd been really unwell, and I'd just gone back to school. I came home after my first day back and went to my room. I'm looking out of my bedroom window and watching both my parents go off to work night shifts. I can see their backs, walking away. I think I learned at that moment that if anyone is going to look after me, it's me. I may be small and needy, but I'm on my own. So, my message from here to little me is, "That can't be right! I've had enough of living by that motto."

Commentary

Through creating the recurrent dream image and allowing the internal dynamic to emerge through speaking from role, the client has gained spontaneous access to an early memory and a driving core belief. The memory itself is the equivalent of a locus scene, a time in her early life when her internal working model was being consolidated. In role analytic terms, the context is a situation where she is vulnerable and in need of care. Her behaviour is that she returns to what should be her secure base, her home. Instead of receiving comfort and connection, she is faced with an image and experience of implicit abandonment, watching her parents' backs as they both leave for work. Her feelings are sadness, forlornness and helplessness. In an attempt to make sense of the situation and to survive the emotional desolation, she comes to believe that when she is in need, she is on her own, that she cannot rely on others to take care of her or be there for her. The consequence is that she develops low expectations of relationships and an image of herself as someone cast adrift on an existential lake of aloneness.

Moving between techniques

I favour a fluidity of approach to dream work in the one-to-one setting. In the examples above, we have explored the brief use of embodied role work and scene setting in Max's session, the use of concretisation on the communicube and a combination of narration and speaking from role in Regina's first dream and the use of art making, leading into speaking from role in Regina's recurrent dream image. In each case the exploration through action supports the ongoing dialogic and relational connection with the therapist in the here and now of the session. The use of role analysis as a supporting reflective frame for the therapist helps to create important links between the dream material and the real-life material brought into the sessions from the everyday experience of the client. Apparently disparate narratives are thus revealed to have deep connections. Making these connections more conscious ultimately supports integration and a sense of personal meaning making in the client.

References

Casson, J. (2007). Psychodrama in Miniature. In C. Baim, J. Burmeister, M. Maciel (eds.), *Psychodrama Advances in Theory and Practice*. Routledge.

Leutz, G. (1986). The Psychodramatic Treatment of Dreams. *Group Analysis* 19(2), 139–146.

Moreno, J.L. (1966). Moreno's Philosophical System. In J. Fox (ed.), *The Essential Moreno: Writings on Psychodrama, Group Method, and Spontaneity.* Springer.

Part II

Case studies

The method in action

Chapter 7

Understanding the child's voice
A systemic approach to one-to-one psychodrama psychotherapy

Paula Davies

Introduction

In this chapter I discuss my use of psychodrama techniques with children in one-to-one therapy in schools, and how I adapt the framework of a classical psychodrama structure of warm-up, action and sharing within the one-to-one setting. I use role analysis within the therapy sessions, as well as in my discussions within the wider system, in order to facilitate a shared understanding of what is happening for the child in their wider process. My aim is to keep the voice of the child alive whilst maintaining links with other systems involved. Adults have a certain amount of control within the education system, for example their involvement in the initial decision for the child to engage in therapy. Indeed, their written consent is always required for the therapy to take place. To balance this, I take great care to ensure the voice of the child is present within the therapy sessions and in my discussions within the wider system. This holistic approach assists the development of resilience in the child to manage the real difficulties they are facing in their lives. The hope is that in time, they will move towards a more harmonious way of living in their world and in relationship with others.

The psychodrama structure as container

The therapeutic alliance is acknowledged as crucial in terms of containing the therapeutic process. I believe that our struggles are linked to our relationship with others, so a trusting relationship is paramount in working through relational difficulties. I regard the psychodramatic structure of warm-up, action and sharing as a containing form within which that crucial relationship develops.

Warm-up

In one-to-one therapy I see the warm-up phase as the period of time where clients prepare to explore their inner issues and struggles, to let go of some of their inhibitions, and to develop the spontaneity and trust to explore their inner worlds authentically and creatively:

> When trauma enters our lives we merely exist, and we cannot live as fully as we would wish. Our creativity is stifled at traumatic times but, with encouragement, it can grow and be used to heal the hurt. When this happens, there is a great feeling of joy and satisfaction.
>
> (Bannister, 1997, p. 71)

Children are naturally playful, spontaneous and creative. When a child is referred to me, they are often blocked. This can be due to trauma and an interruption of their natural developmental process. The warm-up phase attempts to enable them to become more connected to these qualities, preparing them to live a freer life. I understand Anne Bannister's use of the word 'encouragement' as the therapist's role in helping the client to warm up to their world. I believe that the warm-up begins right from the moment of making contact in the classroom, where I meet the child before their session. I begin with recognising the tele between us. This is Moreno's term for the energetic connection between two people, be it positive, negative or neutral. I need to be fully present – that is, fully aware and conscious – to experience this truthfully. The tele occurs before the formal sessions begin. The tele may be an indicator of how the relationship between myself and the child may be, as well as how the child presents themself, including defence patterns. For example, I may feel positively towards the child, and the child may exhibit a negative feeling towards me. The negativity presented to me may be communicated by a defence mechanism such as withdrawal.

Once we are in the therapy room, we engage in activities to warm up to the session content. This might be in the form of a game and creative activities to get in touch with a theme and to arouse spontaneity. A popular game is hangman, which develops a playful bond between us, and where the words I am asked to guess lead to a relevant theme for the child. I also offer sociometric exercises to explore the child's feelings around significant relationships. I have noticed that many children really enjoy expressing themselves on imagined (continuum) lines. Here they stand on the line that expresses how they might feel about another person or group of people. It is easier for the child to communicate discomfort by standing on the negative side or end of the line rather than having to try to verbalise their true feelings. I witness these experiences without judgement.

The warm-up to the session might simply be choosing which materials and methods the child wants to use in the session. Whilst choosing the materials, the child warms up to how they want to use them. As each puppet is being selected, their story is already beginning to unfold.

Action

The action stage in a classical group psychodrama relates to the presentation, exploration and reframing of the selected problem. The action is split into scenes, beginning with the first, which explores the given problem that has happened recently, then moving on to the second scene, which explores the same issue with varied content further back in time. This leads to the locus scene, which is when the issue first emerged. The protagonist now can reframe their experience and develop new more functioning roles. The last scene in the action phase is the role training scene. This gives the protagonist the opportunity to practise the newly developed role to take out into the outside world.

In one-to-one therapy the action can follow a similar process over time. This is different to group psychodrama psychotherapy, where it all happens in one session. Within the individual therapeutic process various problems are explored, tracked back to their origination and reframed. The themes arise naturally over time when the child is warmed up and feels safe to bring them. There may be more than one theme present at one time.

In group psychodrama psychotherapy, the action is acted out by other group members, who adopt roles allocated to them by the protagonist. In one-to-one therapy objects, cloths and drawings are used to represent roles to act out the situation given. Mostly, I do not take on roles because if I were playing another character, there would not be a therapist present, holding the space safely. When I do play a character in the action, I create a separate space in the room for the action to take place. There is always part of the room separated from this, with a chair representing myself as me, the therapist in the here and now. Whenever I sit on this chair, I am back to being myself.

Children engage in their real-life issues in action, as well as fictitious stories and scenarios. The fiction creates a safe emotional distance for the child to explore their vulnerable feelings. In time, the child recognises the connection to their own real-life stories. This work enables them to find a way to make sense of confusing feelings and thoughts. Children often choose puppets to tell their story, as well as art work, mini world sculpting and known stories. Children also embody roles to act out their scenarios on a stage area that we carefully create.

Sharing

The sharing phase of a classical group psychodrama occurs at the end of the enactment, at which point all members of the group de-role from the roles they played. The group has an opportunity to express how the work has impacted them through role feedback and personal sharing. It is a time for self- disclosure and reflection. In one-to-one sharing the therapist does not self-disclose.

In one-to-one therapy with children the sharing is a time for children to reflect on their experience of the session, including what they did and did not enjoy. They might identify aspects of themselves from characters explored. For example, a child who is a young carer, working with Cinderella, might resonate with feelings of being too responsible for others. This phase of the session offers reflective time and a return to the here and now, once all props have been de-roled.

The psychodramatic structure contains each session. The familiar and predictable structure of the one-to-one psychodrama session offers containment, which contributes to trust and a sense of safety. Since the child comes from a classroom and returns to the classroom, it is important that vulnerabilities explored in action are left in the session to a good extent.

Psychodramatic techniques

Moreno created and developed psychodrama after observing and participating with children playing in a park in Vienna (Blatner, 2000). He noticed how children naturally communicated through games and how spontaneous they could be in the roles they played. The birth of psychodrama began with children. When working with trauma and distress, the element of play encourages spontaneity, which assists in resolving stuck patterns.

Moreno devised specific techniques to expand a person's role repertoire. His role theory is used to explore and work through complex issues. The roles played stem from both our internal world and our relationship with others.

The psychodramatic structure of warm-up, action and sharing creates the container of a session within which specific psychodrama techniques can be used. I focus here on the three main techniques used: 'doubling', 'mirror' and 'role reversal'. These are closely linked to children's emotional development. I have paid attention to how they can be adapted and facilitated in one-to-one therapy with children.

Doubling

Doubling is the stage when the infant and caregiver are as if one person. During this stage the infant discovers that they have a separate identity to their caregiver. Doubling as a technique is when the therapist or group member, in group psychodrama psychotherapy, takes the physical position of the client and communicates what they feel might be happening for the client in that moment. It can help by supporting the client to express their inner world more easily as well as helping them understand what is happening for them.

If a child is asked in the school setting why they have behaved aggressively, it can be difficult for them to answer as they often do not know. Doubling, within a therapy session, can contribute to the child gaining a clearer insight into their behaviours, by identifying their feelings and thoughts and accessing words for them. The behaviour is more likely to change when the child has more of an awareness of their experience and is more able to express themself clearly.

Adam Blatner uses the term 'active empathy' (Blatner, 1996) for doubling, as it is empathy in action. The child tends to experience doubling in this way and feel understood. There might be a moment in a therapy session when a child is hiding under a table. At such a time, if they allow, I crawl under the table to be with them and double them in order to gain an empathic understanding of their experience and attempt to enhance my connection with them. I ask if the statement I have made is true for them and invite them to either correct me or put what I am saying in their own words. Children begin to understand that I am present and want to understand them. When this happens, the child is very likely to come out from under the table. The relationship of doubling is analogous to the very early communication between parent and child. The experience of the child is that they are not separate from the mother, and in an ideal setting the mother attunes with the infant's needs and lends herself to expressing these before the child is fully able to do so for themself. Such a relationship forms the foundation for trust and a feeling of safety. Often, my clients have not had this ideal experience in their early life, so it can be deeply reparative for the therapist to provide good doubling in the therapy setting.

I share the doubling technique with other professionals involved with children I work with. It deepens their understanding of why some children cannot relate with others very easily. Doubling helps them understand and develop compassion for children. When an adult understands through the doubling what is behind the child's behaviour, they begin to feel differently about the child, and indeed communicate differently with them. When appropriate, I also share the understanding I have gained through doubling with parents and caregivers to encourage an emotional understanding of their children. It can encourage them to reframe their thinking about their children and the dynamics exhibited in the home.

At any point in the session the child might experience a moment when they feel stuck. There is something happening, but they cannot express it. I can see that something is troubling them, and it feels important to be alongside them. Perhaps something is bothering them from an incident in the classroom or playtime. I use doubling at such points to help us both make sense of their difficulties, and similarly in moments of reluctance or ambivalence to leave at the end of the session. Here a doubling statement might be: 'I don't want to go to the classroom as I have had such a good time here, but I know I will come back next week.'

There are numerous ways to use the double technique with children. When working with children who have great difficulty in focusing, we begin by drawing around each other's hands, cutting the shapes out and creating a chain by threading wool through them. We then guess what our hands like doing. We double the paper hands. With one of my hands on a paper hand, I might say, 'I like drawing.' The child acknowledges or corrects this statement. A process like this warms the child up to being more aware of their emotional experience in the moment. We might move on to feet and other parts of the body before exploring their emotional and internal world. Eventually, children become more focused and their ability to be still vastly improves.

Another example of the use of doubling is when a child makes a puppet. Children enjoy the 'doing' phase of creating a puppet, but they may find it difficult to engage with the personality and emotions of the puppet. This is another opportunity to practise doubling, to encourage the child to explore the inner world of their puppet, and thereby develop the ability to explore their own. I also use doubling with stories we create, or stories already written. We might explore how Little Red Riding Hood experiences her fears and emotional pain by my use of doubling in a scene where the child in role as Little Red Riding Hood is confronted with the confusing image of the wolf impersonating her grandmother.

Another opportunity for doubling is when children draw pictures of themselves. By taking a mental note of facial expressions drawn, I will double the image on the page. I may invite the child to embody the physical position of what they have drawn. This might be the first time the child has felt able to wholly experience and communicate how a situation is for them.

Mirror

Mirroring is the next stage in the emotional development of children. This happens easily if the doubling phase has been managed well. At this point the infant recognises their separateness from their caregiver (Bannister, 1997).

When a child returns to school after a period of absence, they may have a notion that aspects of their school life have changed. New games are being played and new friendships formed. This is perfectly natural in school life and is not necessarily hostile, although the child may experience it this way. The child's peers may have welcomed them back warmly. If the child is not sufficiently mirrored by the school staff, the child's sense of hostility in the other may be accentuated. The child might even believe that the subtle changes are evidence of bullying. If the adult can introduce the child to the reality of the situation with warmth and care, this mirroring will help them feel more at ease.

In group psychodrama psychotherapy, mirroring is the technique used when the protagonist witnesses a scene that they are part of from another perspective outside of the scene. It can be very useful when the protagonist is overwhelmed whilst in the scene, and can help them gain a broader and more realistic viewpoint from watching it this way.

Mirroring is also effective in one-to-one therapy with children. Many of the creative techniques we use enable children to witness their stories from outside themselves. We can use a variety of methods, including art work, stories and puppet work, mini world sculpts, and spectograms with objects such as pebbles and buttons. If we are working with the theme of family, buttons might be chosen to represent family members. It works in the same way if children draw their families. Using this method, they can begin to witness their family dynamics and develop an understanding of their connections and emotional response to what is going on around them. The mirror technique helps them become aware of their position in the family and how it affects them. This way of working might reflect and illuminate a tricky situation happening in the home. If a child does not feel included in a family activity, we can highlight this from the mirror position. They now recognise the situation and may begin to understand why they feel alone. With the child's consent, I may sensitively discuss this with the parents to aid their understanding of how their child experiences themself within their family system. Even if the parent does not agree with this view of this situation, such a conversation may help them develop a compassionate comprehension of the child's perspective and increase their empathy towards the child.

Role reversal

The developmental stage of role reversal is when the child has awareness of other people, and not only themself. Other people's needs can be borne in mind. Empathy is achieved. This is the stage that takes place when the mirroring stage has been good enough. This developmental theory may help us understand why a child has difficulties in unstructured times. Using role reversal, clients learn how to exist in social situations and tolerate any discomfort present. It is about understanding another person's perspective, even if it is different to our own.

In group psychodrama, role reversal involves a person stepping out of their own role and stepping into the role of another. A client could be role reversing with another group member or a significant person in their lives, represented by a group member. We also role reverse with our internal roles, and a group member may represent an internal aspect of self. This develops a richer understanding of how we experience our inner worlds.

In one-to-one therapy with children there is not another person to role reverse with. Therefore, we use inanimate objects to represent the role, be it another person or an internal part of self. These objects include chairs, cloths, puppets, small objects and illustrations. When I work with role, I may use the same structure or activities as when I focus on double or mirror. In a drawing of a family I will invite the child to take on the role of another family member by placing a finger on the person chosen whilst speaking as if they were them. They remain in their role for as long as they have physical contact with their drawing. It works in a similar way if we are using mini world sculpting.

Role reversal can be valuable in story work. A child chooses a character, and we explore their world by role reversing with the other characters around them. For example, by exploring aspects of the Cinderella story by role reversing with the ugly sisters, a child may learn experientially that the sisters were envious of Cinderella's beauty. The child develops some empathic understanding of the ugly sisters and what might be motivating their brutality to Cinderella. The child mentalises them. I have witnessed several children living in a blended family using the Cinderella story in this way to work through the challenge of living with step-siblings. Through role reversal with the fictional characters in the story, the child may come to understand that they are not to blame for the conflict around them. At the same time, they come to realise that the situation is also difficult for their step-siblings.

Children often attach themselves to one puppet, often an aggressive one. The child gives me a more submissive puppet to work with. The child then plays with their chosen puppet for several weeks, expressing their anger and aggression or the anger and aggression they are facing in their lives. I improvise the counter-role with my puppet, and the child corrects me if needed. Once the child has played out their act hunger, they might be ready to role reverse with the puppet I am using. The puppets are used to represent both external and internal role rela-tionships in both their functional and their dysfunctional aspects. Through bringing unconscious dynamics into consciousness, the child has the opportunity to develop more functional roles. For example, I have played the submissive rabbit puppet, whilst the child has played with the aggressive shark. In time the child has played out their aggres-sion and we have swapped puppets. Through this role reversal, the child, in the role of the rabbit, was able to identify the emotional pain the shark experienced beneath its anger. The child was now in touch with vulnerable feelings previously masked by aggression and was beginning to integrate their inner rabbit and shark.

I have given some examples of my use of the basic techniques of double, mirror and role reversal. In the creative process of the session these tech-niques are not used in isolation, and both the child and therapist may initi-ate a transition from one technique to another. It is helpful for me as a psychotherapist to bear in mind the significance and potential impact of each technique in terms of child development.

Role analysis and systemic working

I find role analysis invaluable in one-to-one work with children. It was developed from Moreno's role theory. I reflect on the various stories, fictional and from real life, that the child brings into the sessions in terms of the five elements of role analysis. I consider the same reflective frame to consider the meaning of their difficulties outside of the session in the wider setting of home or school. Here are the five elements:

1. *context* – the situation and presenting issue to which the child responds;
2. *behaviours* – the behaviours displayed and identified in response to the presenting issue;
3. *feelings* – the feelings activated at the time;
4. *belief system* – what the person believes about themself, others and the world in the context presented;
5. *consequence* – this is what happens when the above elements come into play.

One example of using role analysis is with a child experiencing very problematic playtimes at school. He always wanted control of what game was to be played with his peers. If the other children did not want to play his game, the child would become aggressive and physically hurt the others. This repeated scenario was brought to my attention by teachers, meal time assistants and the child himself.

Initially in our sessions I agreed to play some of the games the child wanted to play with his peers. By allowing the child to play his own games, I began to understand that this was giving him a sense of validation and self-worth. His act hunger to be the role of 'game inventor' and 'game controller' was met. Through this process, I learned that he needed to feel in control in order to manage his fear and anxieties of not winning and not knowing the game.

In time I began to introduce my own games. Sensitively and slowly I was encouraging him to let go of his need to control. Further into his process we explored the dynamics in the playground with his peers by creating a similar story to his own. We used role reversal with his playground peers and he told the story of playtime from their perspective. This developed his understanding of the impact of his behaviour on his peers.

In group psychodrama psychotherapy a role analysis is established in one session, based on the protagonist's exploration of their contract and what is explored in each scene. We work towards the locus scene where the belief system that drives the behaviour and feelings is addressed and reframed. In one-to-one therapy a role analysis is usually identified over a series of sessions. It can be possible that we are working with more than one role analysis at a time. This illuminates how we can behave, feel and think differently in a variety of situations. Here is the role analysis that was developed over several weeks with the child in discussion:

> Context – This is a situation where the child is faced with being one of a group of peers all with ideas and impulses about what to play – in other words, faced with the developmental challenge of learning to give and take with his peers.
> Behaviour – He physically attacks one of his peers, shouts, cries and runs away.
> Feelings – He feels angry, anxious, out of control and upset.
> Beliefs – He believes he has to be the one in control or he will be overpowered and overwhelmed. He believes that if people do not do what he says, it means that they do not like him. He believes that the world operates on a dominance or subservience reality.
> Consequence – He isolates himself from others, is punished by the adults and begins to be rejected by his peers.

Sometimes I share a role analysis with children to support their understanding what has been happening for them. If they are receptive to this, we may move on to a deeper exploratory work focused around their belief system. For example, in the case above we were able to explore the origin of his belief that the world operates on a dominance and subservience principle, which was informed by his experience of witnessing domestic abuse at home. I often share the role analysis with other adults connected to the child in and out of school. As with any other sharing, I do need to consider confidentiality at these times. If I feel that it is in the best interest of the child to share with other adults, I will seek the child's consent. The formulation promotes a collective understanding of the child's therapeutic process and how they view the world. There are times when this sharing happens informally. This might be with the class teacher following a session, or if I am working alongside another professional such as a family therapist in a discussion about the family. More usually I share my formulation in informal meetings with other professionals and/or the parents/caregivers. It can be instrumental in informing the direction of the work with the child and/or the family. On the rare occasions when I do not have the child's consent, I will try to include the concept of role analysis in our discussions to encourage the other adults to develop a curiosity about the child's behaviour or presentation, having in mind that I am able to share aspects of the process of the therapy rather than content. Discussions around the role analysis encourage an empathic understanding amongst colleagues and the parents, and enable a systemic approach. In the case of the child discussed above, it became evident that punishing him by keeping him indoors sitting outside the head teacher's office was only colluding with his dysfunctional beliefs about himself. School staff developed a more sympathetic way of working with him. One new intervention was the creation of a 'peer social group' in which he had an opportunity to practise collaboration and give and take within a peer group. This in turn helped improve his negative beliefs about himself. We were able to reflect on this change in his one-to-one therapy sessions.

Antony Williams views human beings in their connectedness with other people (Williams, 1989). If anything is wrong, it means that the connectedness is wrong. He says that working systemically, we should consider the interactions of all relevant members of the system. My work with role analysis aims to ensure more positive connections with all parts of the system, inspired by William's writing.

Children receive labels such as 'naughty', 'greedy' or 'aggressive'. These identities are misguided. The descriptions are roles that are being played in response to specific contexts rather than a definition of who the child is. These labels are heavy burdens contributing to the child's negative belief about themselves. These negative beliefs can be carried forward into their future unless there are adequate therapeutic and systemic interventions. Role analysis assists in thinking about how we think about the children and the language we use with them.

Summary

Children referred for therapy are often very vulnerable and emotionally blocked. They present this in their display of dysfunctional behaviours such as acts of aggression and withdrawal. They often exist in chaos. One-to-one psychodrama psychotherapy offers a creative and playful way for the children to explore these unhealthy defences and patterns that are preventing them from maintaining and achieving healthy relationships. Psychodrama techniques and structure provide a container for the chaos. The frame and therapeutic relationship provide space for the child to explore their spontaneity and creativity safely. The psychodramatic structure contains the therapeutic process and provides security to support the child in their vulnerabilities. Role analysis opens the door to understanding the role system of the child and how they experience their lives and relationships. It acts as a guide into the inner dynamics of the child to enable me to support them towards positive change.

I believe that a systemic perspective is important when working with children, although it is not always possible to liaise with all parts of the child's system. At such times individual psychodrama psychotherapy can still help. In this case, the focus is on building resilience, giving the child a reparative experience of being understood and validated, and an opportunity to develop new roles.

When there is successful co-working across the system, we can co-create new patterns of relating informed by a deeper understanding of the child's inner life and their way of seeing themself in relation to the outside world. My passion is to help us see the child for who they are in the here and now, and to move away from falsely labelling young people.

References

Bannister, A. (1997). *The Healing Drama: Psychodrama and Drama Therapy with Abused Children*. New York. Free Association Books.

Blatner, A. (1996). *Acting-In: Practical Applications of Psychodramatic Methods* (third edition). New York. Springer.

Blatner, A. (2000). *Foundations of Psychodrama* (fourth edition). New York. Springer.

Williams, A. (1989). *The Passionate Technique: Strategic Psychodrama with Individuals, Families and Groups*. London. Routledge.

Chapter 8

Our deepest pain

Working with shame in individual psychodrama psychotherapy

Anna Napier

Introduction

When shame is at the core of our deepest pain – and it so often is – it can take hold and become a pernicious block to connecting with others, with far-reaching and debilitating personal consequences. As Phil Mollon poignantly describes:

> Shame involves a hole, a hole where our connection to others should be. In shame, we fall out of the dance, the choreography of the human theatre. And in the deepest depths of shame we fall into a limbo where there are no words but only silence.
>
> (Mollon, 2002, p. 23)

The potent presence of shame in literature and moral tales reflects the important, influential role that it plays in the human condition. In Hans Christian Andersen's famous tale, the Emperor, duped by conmen into believing that he has been dressed in the finest robes, processes under his canopy through the streets of his community entirely naked. Let us role reverse with the Emperor at the moment the small boy shouts, 'But the Emperor has nothing at all on': the exposure of personal inadequacy and the resulting inner turmoil is the very essence of shame. It is this painful, personal resonance that gives the story its power.

Moreno knew well that our emotional well-being is directly correlated with our experience of connectedness with others and the devastating emotional consequences of being excluded from social groups. He reached out to the social isolates of this world, engaging with their hardship and pain, attempting to reconnect them to a network of relationships (Fox, 1987, p. xv).

One of the defining concepts of psychodrama is Moreno's theoretical stance that the self develops from available roles. In this model, shame can be viewed as a role, one among many, neither good nor bad. The focus of a psychodrama psychotherapist is not to eliminate shame in the client, but rather to understand its meaning, function and purpose and to incorporate it into an ever-expanding repertoire of roles. In this model, the destructive, alienating effects of shame can be acknowledged while also understanding that the capacity to feel shame is an essential part of being human and a member of society.

Uncovering and working with shame in psychotherapy is a sensitive, complex and potentially powerful process. Shame touches deeply the lives of many clients who seek help in therapy, yet its elusive nature can mean that it escapes the attention of both therapists and clients (Lewis, 1971). Perhaps because of the universal personal resonances it evokes, it is one of those areas that therapists might be tempted to avoid.

In this chapter I explore shame in the context of role theory, Moreno's theoretical offering to psychotherapy. I aim to show that role theory, role analysis and the method of psychodrama provide a framework through which to understand and work with shame, whilst keeping hold of its restorative potential. Clinical examples will be used to illustrate how shame can be identified, validated and recalibrated within our internal role system using a role analytic framework in the context of the individual therapeutic encounter.

What is shame?

Shame is a tender, sometimes painful and distressing emotion, immediately and viscerally felt in the physical body, As Jean-Paul Sartre described: 'it is an immediate shudder which runs through me from head to foot without any discursive preparation' (2003, p. 246). Shame is rooted in our sense of who we are and how we are seen. This duality of the private and social elements of shame has evolutionary origins. Gilbert (2011) places shame firmly within the evolutionary drive to maintain social bonds. The function of shame is to alert the self to the threat of disconnection from others. It is an important emotional signal to alter behaviour to ensure survival via continued inclusion in the group. In ordinary social interactions shame may arise when there are changes in others' responses that indicate a loss of emotional connection. For example, one of my clients spoke about an incident in which shame drew her attention sharply to address an uncomfortable dynamic.

Marie, a mother, was complaining to other parents in a heated manner about the class teacher. Marie noticed a disapproving frown from one parent and saw another look to the floor. Observing that the other parents did not support her position, and sensing their emotional withdrawal, she felt shame, a jolt of pain alerting her to the potential for rejection and the need to adjust her tone of communication.

This capacity to recognise emotions and read social cues is developed in early childhood, beginning with facial mirroring exchanges between infants and caregivers. Winnicott describes the origins of how the sense of self develops when the infant looks into the mother's face: '*What she looks like is related to what she sees there*' (1971, p. 112, emphasis in the original). In psychodynamic readings of shame, repeated failures in early mirroring interactions are viewed as the foundations of chronic shame in later life. The primary caregiver may be preoccupied, disinterested or depressed, the infant is left adrift, unable to get their needs met via the expression of emotion.

There is now a wealth of research in the field of developmental neuroscience that supports the psychodynamic emphasis on the significance of the mother–infant dyadic relationship and its influence on the growth of the brain. Schore (2016) suggests that a caregiver's failure to regulate the transmission of shame can have damaging consequences for a child's developing brain. For example, in the process of socialisation, a caregiver might respond to a toddler's behaviour by saying 'No' or 'Stop' accompanied by a facial expression that invokes shame in the toddler. A responsive caregiver will reach out to re-establish connection, returning the toddler to a state of positive affect through facial mirroring and physical contact. The key to the development of self-regulatory capacities, says Schore, lies in this *essential process of repair of the shame experience*. He writes:

> The experience of being with a regulating (or dysregulating) other is incorporated into an enduring interactive representation. Such representations can be accessed in the future in order to autoregulate shame states.
>
> (Schore, 2016, p. 248)

According to Schore, the roots of many psychosomatic illnesses and other developmental psychopathologies lie in prolonged experiences of misattunement and failures to regulate shame in early life.

The sense of struggle and hopelessness to create relationships in which needs can be met and reciprocated is characteristic of the shame-prone clients in my practice, the absence of attuned, empathetic parental responses having left them in a chronic state of learned helplessness in relation to the deep human need for connection.

Shame and other emotions

When clients seek help, they are often unclear about what is troubling them, confused about why they feel anxious or low in mood. Almost never will they name 'shame' as a central issue. As Miller (1993) explains, we do not naturally put complex emotional states into words until we have fully developed and understood their significance in the context of our experience. This is one of the tasks of psychotherapy.

Emotions, then, help us to make sense of experience.

When the ability to identify and express nuances of emotion is enabled through attuned mirroring within the therapeutic process, the client is in a better position to identify and express their real human needs. The therapeutic endeavour may be helpfully assisted by making subtle distinctions between shame and other emotions.

Following Wurmser's (1981) definition of shame as a 'family of emotions', affect theorist Nathanson describes the spectrum of emotional experience that ranges from 'the mildest twinge of embarrassment to the searing pain of mortification' (1992, p. 19). Anxiety is often a presenting feature of shame, signalling the underlying fear of exposure that accompanies the unspoken 'keep out' message that emanates from clients with high levels of shame. Anger frequently arises as a defensive strategy to protect the self from acknowledging and feeling the paralysing impact of shame (Morrison, 2011).

Miller (1993) differentiates shame and embarrassment. Like shame, embarrassment can be experienced alone as well as with others, but it is accompanied by a felt sense of involuntary exposure that is situational. The transition into shame occurs when the agony of being seen is accompanied by negative self-evaluation, for example: 'I slipped and fell over and I felt so silly' (embarrassment), 'They all saw me for the idiot I am' (shame). Several authors make a conceptual distinction between shame and guilt. Essentially, this distinction is the evaluation of self in shame compared with a specific behaviour in guilt. Shame is associated with a sense of personal inadequacy, whereas guilt involves the recognition of some behavioural violation (Dearing and Tangney, 2011). It is the difference between 'I got too angry with my kids and I need to acknowledge I overreacted, say sorry and make it up to them' (guilt) and 'There I go again, I'm a bad mother, unworthy of being a parent' (shame).

For my client Nina, the process of naming the role of shame and acknowledging how it had taken hold of her life was a crucial step towards improving her relationship with her children. Having grown up with a severely depressed mother, Nina had learnt to suppress her emotional needs and to gain attention by pleasing others. When she had her own children, the absence of attuned mothering in her own childhood left her struggling to contain her children's emotional ups and downs and she would frequently become angry and punitive towards them. She turned her focus to working long hours and filling her spare time engaging in charity events to impress others. This led to her repeating the same pattern of emotional disengagement from her children as she had experienced from her mother. The role of shame was named in the session as we explored together her reluctance to look at her emotional neglect of her children. Once we had identified the shame, she became more able to embrace the role of guilt, which in turn facilitated authentic reparative encounters with her children.

Shame in the individual setting

Shame in therapy presents in a variety of ways. Some expressions of shame are more easily identifiable, visibly expressed in the body and speech, while others are hidden behind carefully constructed defences.

A young woman enters the therapy room for the first time, she fleetingly attempts eye contact with me, then immediately collapses her gaze. Her body is hunched uncomfortably on the edge of the chair, a physical sign of the presence of shame in the room. Another client recounts a story of overhearing children in the street mocking her size. She has a barely audible voice, she swallows between words and brings her hands to her face. I notice the tension in my muscles and resist what feels like a silent invitation to avert my eyes. The familiar gesture of covering the face and the story content of humiliation indicates we will almost certainly be working with shame. Another client gives a dazzlingly detailed account of his academic achievements and his superior status at work. The litany of accomplishments he delivers is in stark contrast to the absence of any meaningful relationships in his life, and do not compensate for his desperate struggle to feel he is loveable. Even I, his therapist, am not allowed to see behind the mask of competence where feelings of unworthiness, loneliness and despair are hiding, rooted in a childhood story of abuse and loss. Another client repeatedly complains that he doesn't trust my methods or ability to keep him safe. He says: 'I've been coming for months and nothing has changed.' I feel defensive, my hackles are rising, my inner voice simultaneously critical of the client for blocking my attempts to connect and alerting me to a sense of my own inadequacy. The role of the self-doubter has been evoked in me and takes prominence in my internal role system. I struggle to think of an adequate response, and make a clumsy attempt to reassure him that he is safe. On reflection, I make sense of this interaction as projective identification in which the client's feeling of shame is successfully projected into me.

Another client arrives fraught with anxiety and stress following a shocking and pernicious public shaming on social media of an incident in which he is exposed as having fallen from grace. He tells me that nightmares punctuate otherwise sleepless nights and racing thoughts about his inevitable rejection from professional life and a career left in tatters preoccupy his days. My anger at the injustice of his predicament pulls me towards a collusion with his rageful tirade against the parties who instigated his downfall and the persecutory social environment that supports it. At the same time as validating his anger, I am conscious that the vital work will be in healing the internal wound of shame and its crushing impact on his relationship with himself.

Role theory, role analysis and shame

At the heart of psychodrama theory is Moreno's assertion that the self is constituted from roles. Role is 'the functioning form the individual assumes in the specific moment he reacts to the specific situation in which other person or objects are involved' (Moreno, 1964, p. iv, in Fox, 1987, p. 62).

A unique and defining concept of role theory is that roles are situational, they arise according to the perception and meaning that is given to a specific context. The context, then, is what defines the personal and social relevance a role has for self-evaluation (Van Dijk, 2008). This idea is helpful in understanding role responses that involve complex emotions like shame. Firstly, the specific details of the situations that bring about shame are crucial in understanding the meaning it holds for each person. When shame is triggered, the roles that are accessed tend to be those habitually utilised in similar contexts. Common shame behaviours are to disengage, to appease others, to become critical, angry or take a superior position to mask self-critical thoughts. When the context is one that resonates with historical trauma, the threat of exclusion, rejection or loss in status overwhelms the client and they retreat into the 'safety' of a familiar role response regardless of the consequences.

The London Centre for Psychodrama Group and Individual Psychotherapy teaches a framework for analysing roles drawn from the work of Antony Williams (1989) and Dalmiro Bustos (2004). This begins with a formulation of the problematic roles in the here and now. Williams identifies five components of role: context, behaviour, belief, feeling and consequences. The origins, or locus, of the role are then tracked, determining the time and place the role first came into being.

The same role analytic structure can be applied in the individual therapy setting. The formulation of a problematic role response may take place over many sessions. It is likely to be a more subtle, nuanced process going back and forth between here and now and past experiences. As clients reveal their stories, this framework allows therapist and client to begin unravelling the complexity of shame, breaking down the felt experience into role elements that can be more easily grasped.

A role analytic approach to shame

Taking a role analytic stance involves a detailed exploration of the context, the situation in which the role of shame emerges. I ask focused questions to elicit the conditions and circumstances that precipitate the role response. The context defines whether a role response is adequate, underdeveloped or overdeveloped. When exploring problematic scenarios that involve shame with clients, it is almost always shame that is the overdeveloped role, overpowering underdeveloped or depleted roles that relate to self-worth, self-confidence and compassion for self and others. Where shame permeates, the context will always have both interpersonal and intrapsychic elements, whether the role response is to an actual social situation or the presence of imaginary judging others in the client's mind. Analysis of the client's behaviour includes both internal and external behavioural aspects.

The pain of shame typically gives rise to avoidant behaviours to reduce the threat of further exposure or exclusion. This can lead to incongruence between internal and external behaviour – for example, clients who appear successful and competent but internally attack the self. These critical, demeaning self-judgements are characteristic of shame behaviours. I take time to identify and name the different feelings, putting words to the experience of shame. This often requires patience and persistence, as clients will often speak in generalised terms, such as 'I just feel so bad', or use metaphors to capture the intensity and significance of the feeling. I search for the underlying beliefs that drive the behaviour. I listen for messages about the self as inadequate or worthy of rejection, or others as critical, belittling or dismissive. Investigating the consequences of a role first involves understanding its function and what motivates the client to maintain it. In shame, this relates to the belief that the self must be protected from further exposure or rejection. This may need to be acknowledged and validated alongside identification of other detrimental consequences which may seem irrelevant to the client in the moment. In many instances, this will involve disconnection from others and an exacerbation of negative shaming messages about the self.

Clinical examples

Working with words: Jane and the role of the shameful hider from conflict

In the following example, the work is entirely a verbal exchange informed by role theory and role analysis.

Jane was discussing difficulty in her work, where she asks for help with a task and instead receives what she perceives as harsh and critical feedback from her supervisor (*context*). She tries to convey her own perception of the issue to her boss, but stumbles over her words and is ignored. She gives up trying to express herself and stays silent, politely saying she is grateful for the helpful comments. She attacks herself for making mistakes (*internal behavioural role response*) and goes to the bathroom to hide (*external behaviour*). She feels fear and an overwhelming sense of shame (*feelings*). She believes that it is dangerous to express herself, that others want to cause her harm by exposing her inadequacies and are deliberately withholding support. In addition, she perceives herself to be trapped and helpless to do anything about it (*belief*). She is left unable to complete the task she had asked for help with and cancels her evening social plans, ruminating in her room about ways to leave her job (*consequences*).

For Jane it became clear that her behaviours were desperate attempts to prevent further shaming experiences, regardless of the consequences. The naming of her feelings in the therapy session brought about an emotional catharsis expressed in tears of sadness and grief. In subsequent sessions we identified several other examples in her present life where shame overwhelms Jane, in each case the context is similarly where her attempts to express herself are shut down by others leading to her desperate wish to disappear and hide away.

Jane described a series of incidents as a child where she refused to go out in the car with her family. Her father would ignore her protests (*context*) and drag her from under her bed while she kicked and screamed in desperation. He would then force her into the back of the car with her sister, who joined in the family bullying. In recounting the story in the therapy session, she recoiled in her chair and impulsively brought a cushion to cover her face as if to shield herself from the deep shame she felt so palpably in the space between us. Jane had no words for her feelings as a child, instead describing her repeated experiences of powerlessness in the face of belittling messages from her father in metaphor: 'I felt like I was standing alone in the middle of Wembley stadium, the whole crowd staring at me like I was a bad person.' In this moment, the belief that to express her authentic feelings, thoughts and needs will be ineffective, exposing and shaming was firmly instilled in Jane. Her use of metaphor captures precisely the way public and private dimensions coincide in shame experiences.

We discussed how Jane's here and now role had emanated from a hiding role in her early childhood which she could now see was a creative and protective role response to the volatile and aggressive atmosphere of her childhood family home. She used to find places to hide alone in the hope that no one would find her. Jane had learnt that the only way to protect herself was to make herself invisible.

Working with action: concretisation, role reversal and the meta-role: Jon and the 'self-critic'

At the heart of the psychodrama method is the process of symbolising experience. When we concretise our internal role system, we shine a light on what is 'in here' and put it 'out there' so we can facilitate a vantage point from which to understand, manipulate and recalibrate our internal world. The complex dynamics of shame are more easily explored when there is distance and it can be seen in concrete form. The client can then be invited to role reverse with parts of the sculpt we create in the therapy space. This intervention often helps clients access feelings of which they were previously unaware. Moreno called this 'action-insight' (Kellerman, 1992).

The choice to offer an intervention of concretisation or role reversal emerges spontaneously for me during the dialogue of a session. The structure of a session may not follow the same shape as in classical group psychodrama. I try to stay attuned to moments of authentic feeling in the client's narrative. When I pause and offer an action-based intervention, I am taking the opportunity to mark or expand a particular aspect of the work. I listen carefully for progressive roles and seize the moment to symbolise these.

I frequently draw on Adam Blatner's concept of the 'meta-role'. Blatner emphasises the managerial function of this role, 'a part that analyses and decides how the various roles should be played' (Blatner, 2007, p. 53).

The meta-role is a useful technique when complex internal role elements are at play. This is especially true when entrenched overdeveloped shame roles persist. Where there is shame, there is always the role of the self-critic that denigrates the self with put-down messages. This role can also hide behind criticism of others, and it is common in shame to see clients vacillate between both parts of this role.

In the following example, internalised critical role relationships are explored using concretisation, role reversal and the meta-role.

Jon frequently began sessions with a heated litany of complaints about his colleagues at work. In one session he spoke about his boss having been critical of his performance while praising his younger colleagues. The scene was set up using five chairs and objects to represent the different external and internal roles. The context is represented by the boss (chair 1) and the colleagues (chair 2). We then explored Jon's emotional experience, using objects to concretise feelings of anxiety, rage and fear of rejection. We identified a parallel internal behavioural role pattern and placed two chairs side by side to represent the two faces of the role. These were the 'critical of others' role (chair 3) and the 'critical of self' role (chair 4). In role reversal we explored the conflictual relationship between the dual elements of this internal role in more depth.

In role reversal as 'critical of others' we see Jon ruminating about how mean and useless his boss is and giving several examples of 'far worse' mistakes made by his colleagues (*internal behaviour*). This serves to quieten the shaming internal 'critical of self' role that delivers denigrating messages towards himself: 'you are incompetent, and you deserve to lose your job … you don't belong here' (*belief*). In response to this, Jon shows us how he avoids a direct encounter with his boss, instead sending emails with contemptuous belittling remarks (*external behaviour*). I then invited him to role reverse with his meta-role (chair 5). From this vantage point he immediately recognised that the role that criticises others serves to protect him from experiencing the full velocity of the self-critical role that shames him. Jon also articulated the negative impact of the role: he is excluded from team meetings and social events. His anxiety is exacerbated, and consequently he has difficulty sleeping. He sees that his persistent ruminating does reduce the intensity of the shame momentarily, but he is left exhausted and unable to effectively function in the days ahead (*consequences*).

In subsequent sessions we explored the historical context in which this role pattern emerged, his violent alcoholic father and a mother who colluded with father's aggressive criticism of him, constantly comparing him to his

114   Anna Napier

younger brother who in their eyes could do no wrong. This helped Jon to recognise he had introjected the critical and collusive parents and their shaming messages. In this powerful transference of situation, the celebrated colleagues represented his favoured brother.

I wondered with him if we might introduce the role of compassion. He agreed, but resisted inhabiting this role, perhaps because, as Gilbert (2011) suggests, it can be painful to get in touch with the grief of the compassion we have never had. In the 'as if' of the meta-role, he could acknowledge the need to show kindness towards himself and strengthening this role became a core element of future work.

From action to words – creating a narrative: Mary

Putting experience into words is a symbolic process that allows us to create distance, perspective and meaning. When analysing a role response, careful attention is given to naming the constituents within each of the five role elements, but this can be a slow and painstaking venture for some clients for whom verbal forms of communication are not readily accessible. Traumatic experience such as physical, sexual or emotional abuse, or consistent failures in mirroring of emotional experience in childhood can block the development of the capacity to verbalise internal experience. As the child develops into adulthood, relational needs may continue to be unacknowledged or pushed away. One role solution to protect the self from the corrosive impact of shame is dissociation, in which intolerable, wordless feelings are split off, hidden not only from others, but also from the self (Stadter, 2011).

In this example, my client Mary was cut off from conscious awareness of her feeling states and became a hoarder, surrounding herself with objects and furniture. Four action-based interventions are used to help her to access words to describe her internal experience; the use of art materials, the use of the 'as if', the containing double and the mirror.

Mary, a 37-year-old single woman had been referred for psychotherapy by her GP after complaining to her doctor that she was being bullied by her next-door neighbour. The neighbour had safety concerns about her hoarding and had threatened to call the police and fire brigade if Mary didn't clear her 'junk', now spilling out of her back door.

Early therapy sessions with Mary involved little eye contact, long silences broken by blank expressions of her desire to 'give up on life'. When asked what she would like to focus on in therapy, she would say, 'I don't know, I just feel stuck, my life is pointless … my GP said it might help to talk.' She made scathing remarks about her neighbour, convinced that he thought she was a 'nobody' and was intent on turning the authorities against her so she would be evicted from her flat. I suspected that beneath her protestations she was deeply ashamed of herself and the way she lived, the neighbour holding the projection of her punishing self-hatred.

Behind her hostile comments that her neighbour wanted to 'drive her out', she also expressed her fear that she would be evicted from her home. She felt overwhelmed by the amount of clutter mounting in her flat, there was little space to store the things she bought, and she couldn't keep her flat clean. She recognised the problems were escalating, yet she felt unable to tidy, scale down her belongings or curtail her spending.

For Mary there was little felt connection between her external behaviour and her inner world. I viewed this through the lens of Bateman and Fonagy's (2006) model of mentalisation, where failures in marked and contingent mirroring in early life lead to a deficit in the capacity to access words to describe internal experience. For example, she described how every Sunday she went to house clearance markets and car boot sales and bought things from stalls stacked full of furniture and bric-a-brac. She could not give a clear account of the underlying feelings and beliefs that motivated her to continue buying objects for which she had no apparent need. She would say: 'I like a bargain' or 'It gets me out and about'. Similarly, she had no idea of what blocked her attempts to tidy her flat and seemed cut off from associated feelings.

Use of art materials

I wanted to bring Mary's flat into the therapeutic space so that she could show me the problem and emotional dilemmas surrounding her hoarding with more immediacy. Sensing the potential for Mary to feel overwhelmed, and thus be retraumatised, it was important to offer some symbolic distance. I suggested she use art materials to create a scaled-down visual representation of her flat, anticipating that this would be sufficiently containing for Mary to safely explore the problematic roles in more detail.

I used a large square cloth placed on the floor to mark the space of her flat, clearly demarcated from the therapeutic space concretised by our respective chairs. I then placed a large piece of paper on the cloth and, using coloured crayons, pencils and pens, I asked her to make marks and shapes on the paper to represent the furniture and objects in her room. I asked her to set the scene, marking windows, doors and significant items of furniture and objects to orientate us both to the space of her flat.

With impressive attention to detail, she took great care to ensure that every aspect of her room was visible. I then suggested she place a finger on the significant parts of the picture and asked questions to elicit the meaning they held for her.

Through the pictures, Mary was drawn into the there and then of the stories that surrounded the acquisition of the furniture and objects. I realised that what we were seeing were aspects of Mary, a range of different roles concretely represented in the objects in her room. With no access to language to articulate her internal experience, the hoarding was an expression of who she is, her sense of self, each object symbolising a different role.

For example, she smiled when speaking about an old A-level mathematics text book, 'I was good with numbers, top of the class' (competent, successful self), the heavy blankets that blocked the light from the windows, 'I bought these because I felt sorry for the man selling them out of his ramshackle car, he had lost his wife to cancer ... still, they help block the light from the windows, so the neighbours can't see in' (the role that looks after others, but also the role that doesn't want to be seen) and the CD shelf perfectly ordered from A to Z (the role that can be organised, a 'logical organiser' role).

I was beginning to recognise not only her chaos, but also the richness of her personality.

'As if'

I wondered whether, if I came alongside her, entering the 'as if' of her flat concretised on the cloth, this might help both her and me to connect with the dynamics of her inner role system (the space, clearly marking the frame within a frame). From within the scene we looked together at a large pile of clothing, an area she wanted to address. I asked what would happen if she picked up a shirt and put it away. She stared at the clothes in silence, her body frozen like a rabbit caught in headlights. Under her breath she angrily whispered: 'I just can't – I just want to disappear.' We were now standing together facing her shame response. Sensing her trauma, I suggested she take a step off the cloth and into the mirror position. I stood next to her.

Drawing on Hudgins and Drucker's (1998) concept of the containing double, I offered doubling statements to bring her back into the here and now of the time and place of the therapy room: 'I'm with Anna in the therapy space, we are looking together at the hoarding, I feel so ashamed.'

In terms of the role analysis, these were my reflections.

Faced with the task of tidying and putting away a pile of clothes (*context*), she is frozen, unable to move physically, and does nothing (*behaviour*), she feels a sense of helpless despair alongside intense fear and shame (*feelings*). She believes that her hoarding gives her a sense of identity, and without it she will 'be nothing, a nobody'. She is left in a state of both physical and emotional paralysis, unable to function adequately and engaged in hostile, conflictual relationships with others (*consequences*).

Locus of role

Over many weeks Mary started to put her life story into words that made sense of what we had witnessed together. She had been raised by an alcoholic mother who was a single parent, her father's departure following her birth was unexplained. At the age of 10 she found her mother intoxicated with alcohol, lying unconscious on the kitchen floor. She tried to shake her awake, but to no avail, so she ran to a neighbour, who called an ambulance. Her mother died shortly after arriving at hospital, and Mary was subsequently raised in local authority care. She had lost everything, and although she was cared for with kindness, no one helped her to talk about her traumatic early experiences. The role of hoarding emerged as the only means of expression of her sense of self, filling the empty void left by trauma and an absence of safe caregiving.

Conclusion

The idea that well-being is achieved through connectedness with others is at the heart of Moreno's relational philosophy. When shame dominates, the potential for connection is severely compromised. For clients with prominent shame-related issues, the therapeutic alliance is a necessary precursor to the more in-depth work of analysing the specific shame-related role and its historical origin. Since shame arises in a relational context, an empathic, attuned therapeutic relationship can provide the containing environment necessary for clients to begin to address shame and give the potential to experience trust in both themselves and others. This may take time and a leap of faith from both therapist and client.

Role theory provides a structure that allows access to the complicated internal and external dynamics of shame. The detailed focus of the role analytic approach can be applied in the individual setting using action-based interventions or purely verbal therapeutic exchanges. This can enable overwhelming or hidden experiences of shame to be expressed, deeper meanings to emerge and possibilities for richer relational connections.

References

Bateman, A. and Fonagy, P. (2006) *Mentalization Based Treatment: A Practical Guide*. Oxford, UK: Oxford University Press.

Blatner, A. (2007) 'The role of the meta-role: An integrative element in psychology'. In: C. Baim, J. Burmeister and M. Maciel (Eds). *Psychodrama: Advances in Theory and Practice*. Hove, UK: Routledge.

Bustos, M.D. (2004) 'Wings and roots'. In: P. Holmes, M. Karp and M. Watson (Eds). *Psychodrama Since Moreno: Innovations in Theory and Practice*. London: Routledge.

Dearing, J.P. and Tangney, J.P. (2011) 'Introduction: Putting shame in context'. In: R. L. Dearing and J.P. Tangney (Eds). *Shame in the Therapy Hour*. Washington, DC: American Psychological Association.

Fox, J. (1987) *The Essential Moreno: Writings on Psychodrama, Group Method, and Spontaneity*. New York: Springer.

Gilbert, P. (2011) 'Shame in psychotherapy and the role of compassion focused therapy'. In: R.L. Dearing and J.P. Tangney (Eds). *Shame in the Therapy Hour*. Washington, DC: American Psychological Association.

Hudgins, K. and Drucker, K. (1998) 'The containing double as part of the therapeutic spiral model for treating trauma survivors'. *International Journal of Action Methods*, 51, 2, 63–74.

Kellerman, P.F. (1992) *Focus on Psychodrama: The Therapeutic Aspects of Psychodrama*. London: Jessica Kingsley Publishers.

Lewis, H.B. (1971) *Shame and Guilt in Neurosis*. New York: International Universities Press.

Miller, S. (1993) *The Shame Experience*. Hillsdale, NJ: The Analytic Press.

Mollon, P. (2002) *Shame and Jealousy*. London: Karnac Books.

Morrison, A.P. (2011). 'The psychodynamics of shame'. In: R.L. Dearing and J.P. Tangney (Eds). *Shame in the Therapy Hour*. Washington, DC: American Psychological Association.

Nathanson, D.L. (1992) *Shame and Pride: Affect, Sex and the Birth of the Self*. New York: W.W. Norton.

Sartre, J.P. (2003) *Being and Nothingness: An Essay on Phenomenological Ontology*. London: Routledge.

Schore, A.N. (2016) *Affect Regulation and the Origin of the Self*, New York: Routledge.

Stadter, M. (2011) 'The inner world of shaming and ashamed: An object relations perspective'. In: R.L. Dearing and J.P. Tangney (Eds). *Shame in the Therapy Hour*. Washington, DC: American Psychological Association.

Van Dijk, T.A. (2008) *Discourse and Context: A Sociocognitive Approach*. Cambridge, UK: Cambridge University Press.

Williams, A. (1989) *The Passionate Technique: Strategic Psychodrama with Individuals, Families and Groups*. London: Routledge.

Winnicott, D.W. (1971) 'Mirror role of mother and child in family development'. In: D.W. Winnicott (Ed). *Playing and Reality*. Harmondsworth, UK: Penguin Books.

Wurmser, L. (1981) *The Mask of Shame*. Baltimore, MD: John Hopkins University Press.

Chapter 9

Working with grief and loss

Lydia Mak

In this chapter, I share my experience of the application of psychodrama to work with grief and loss in one-to-one psychotherapy in the context of Hong Kong Chinese culture. When significant relationships are broken, through long separation or death, a person can be prone to depression (Farmer, 1998, p. 243). The depressed person is usually struggling with conflicting emotions and confused thoughts resulting from the unfinished issues with the lost persons. Psychodrama provides opportunities to complete these unresolved interactions.

Mourning and depression

Some bereaved people may develop major depression. Depression can happen when the person is unable to work through their grief and loss. Emotional expression and crying are usually essential and healthy during the grieving process. Failure to mourn their losses may lead to delayed and complicated grief, which may cause a chronic depressive mood.

Suppression of emotional expression in Chinese culture

Though Hong Kong is a place which combines Chinese and Western cultures, for the older generations and those observing a more conservative Chinese culture, death is still a taboo subject today. The more traditional Chinese avoid openly talking about the issue. "Don't wash your dirty linen in public" is a common idiom here, which means private family problems should not be disclosed to outsiders, to preserve "face" for the family. It can be difficult for bereaved Chinese persons, as they have a very strong tendency to suppress their emotional expressions. The expression of feelings towards the deceased like anger, which is so common in grief, may arouse feelings of guilt and be understood as disrespect and unfilial to the dead, even as a form of family disloyalty.

Working with psychodrama in Chinese culture

Psychodrama psychotherapy is useful in helping the emotionally inhibited Chinese to express their feelings and to work through grief and loss. It provides an opportunity for direct emotional expression to the deceased through the method of the psychodramatic encounter. It also provides a channel to support the less direct expression of emotion through the use of concretisation and "spectogram" (miniatures).

I introduce here an example from my one-to-one psychodrama practice. The example is given with the client's consent, while I have changed various identifying features. Let us firstly meet the client, Sue. Sue is a Chinese woman, aged 35, who presented for therapy with a long-standing diagnosis of depression. She had suicidal ideations, with self-harming behaviours. She was also struggling with anxiety, strong self-criticism, and pronounced low self-esteem.

Sue's emotional problems were deeply related to the grief issues in her family. She had had multiple losses in her life. Her father died suddenly in an accident when Sue was 13. Just four years later, when she was 17, her second sister was killed on the spot in a fatal traffic accident in America. Both these deaths took the form of fatal accidents, where there was no preparation for death and no opportunity for Sue to say "good-bye" to them. She did not have the chance to attend her sister's funeral in America, which impacted her ability to work through the loss. Following conservative Chinese culture, emotional expression was not allowed at home. She forced herself to suppress her natural grief responses and pretended that nothing had happened. It enabled her to get on with her life at one level, but her failure to mourn these losses led to delayed and complicated grief, which caused a chronic depressive mood in Sue.

As Sue revealed her story at the beginning of our work together, the wider family perspective proved significant. Her mother was absorbed in her grief and could hardly provide any emotional support to Sue during these difficult times. The mother herself had had suicidal wishes after her husband's sudden death, so Sue did not dare to show any of her grief nor any other negative emotions at that time for fear of triggering her mother's distress. She lived in fear that she would also lose her mother. As is typical in many conservative Chinese families, her family discouraged any expression of emotions. As Sue suppressed all negatively perceived emotions, she gave up trying to understand her feelings and paid the price of losing contact with her sense of self. She started to have suicidal thoughts and engaged in self-harming behaviour since adolescence. She covered up her difficulties in front of others. Multiple loss and unexpressed sadness left her with strong self-attacking internal critics. The price was paid in anxiety, depression, and emptiness, common symptoms for adults with a pathological grief reaction (Leick & Davidsen-Nielsen, 1991, p. 17).

Role analysis

In Sue's situation, her earlier developmental difficulties with object loss were continuously re-evoked in the course of later relationships. Every loss revives an earlier one (Taylor, 2008).

Recently, when Sue's nephew was about to go to America for further studying, her long-suppressed sadness and confused emotions over losing her sister were stirred up. Her 18-year-old nephew was the elder son of her eldest sister, while he was born just a few days after Sue's second sister died in the fatal accident in America. The nephew's choice of studying in America triggered Sue's deep sadness at losing her sister there. As the date of the nephew's departure was approaching, Sue became increasingly anxious, to the point where she started to have suicidal ideations. She worried her nephew would follow the path of her second sister who lost her life there. Sue did not share these worries with her family. When Sue shared her anxieties and fantasies with me, I could feel her intense fear and anxiety built on the deep wounds of her earlier experience of loss.

On the day of the nephew's departure to America, when Sue escorted him to the airport, she only presented her "happy" face in front of the other family members. Only after the nephew had left did Sue cry bitterly, alone in the airport after all the others had gone. Her feelings were intense, not only because of the current separation from her nephew, but even more forcefully because all the feelings associated with the loss of her sister so many years previously were re-evoked.

While role analysis is usually applied in directing classical psychodrama psychotherapy in a group, I also use it in one-to-one work as an assessment of the client's dominant roles in relation to others and particular situations. It provides the client and myself with a more comprehensive understanding of their patterns. There are five key elements in the role analysis: the context in which the role arises, the feelings experienced in the role, the actual behaviour in the situation, the belief system the behaviour is based on, and the consequences of all these for the client. Based on the above situation described by Sue, I used role analysis in the following way.

In Sue's case, role analysis reveals the *context* to be a situation where she is facing separation from a family member. The nephew was embarking on a journey following in the footsteps of his aunt going to America to study. America was also the place where his aunt died during her journey there. Moreover, this nephew was born just a few days after his aunt died in the fatal traffic accident in America. The separation is therefore of a transferential nature for Sue. Her *feelings* are of intense separation anxiety, fear, a sense of helplessness and sadness. Her actual *behaviour* in this situation is to keep her worries to herself. She presents her "happy" face to others. She cries alone, bitterly, and only when her emotions have reached a crescendo of intensity. She also fantasises about killing herself. Her *belief* system seems to include the following. She may believe that her family is fated to experience sudden and accidental death. Going to the country of that death is inviting fate. Sharing her feelings would burden others. The only way to end put an end to her suffering is to kill herself. Moreover, it would be easier for her to die than to witness another family member's death. The *consequences* are that Sue continues to keep her feelings to herself, isolates herself from potential support, and develops self-attacking impulses.

For Sue to understand how her past experiences and belief systems influenced the present day, I decided to help her explore the origins and contributing factors around the irrational belief that her family was fated to die through sudden accidents. As we explored this in the session, we tracked Sue's memory back to the time when her sister had just died. It was the second traumatic death of a significant family member for Sue, and she remembered clearly how at that time she developed a strong wish that it had been herself rather than her sister in the car, or that they at least should have died together. It implied a belief that she has no right to life when her sister has lost hers, or even that Fate has made a mistake and taken the wrong person.

Empty chair dialogue

In the following, I present the use of the psychodramatic technique of empty chair dialogue. I offered Sue the chance to speak with her deceased sister as an opportunity to work through some of her unexpressed feelings. With the support of our strong therapeutic alliance, she was open to trying the technique, which we both knew would be challenging for her. I set out two chairs opposite each other. Sue sat on one chair, while the chair opposite would stand for the role of her sister.

THERAPIST: Do you want to tell your sister the 18-year-old nephew just went to America to pursue studies? Tell your sister how you feel now.

SUE: Our nephew, eldest sister's son, is already aged 18. He just went to America to pursue studies there as you did.

I recognised here that she was struggling to find her words, and offered some doubling suggestions as a prompt.

THERAPIST AS DOUBLE: The nephew was born just a few days before your accident occurred.

Facing the empty chair representing her sister, Sue sat in silence.

THERAPIST: (continuing to try to support her to come into her flow) Tell your sister how much you love her and miss her.

Sue remained silent for a long time and shook her head.

THERAPIST AS DOUBLE: I find it so hard to tell you what is in my heart. It's so difficult to tell you how much I miss you.

SUE: (turning to the therapist) I feel shameful, and I want to hide from facing her (the deceased sister). I don't want my sister to know my secret thoughts.

I recognised the importance for her to express her feelings, but noticed that her inhibition followed her even into the "as if" structure I had set up. Perhaps it implied a belief that even beyond death, her sister could be hurt by the expression of Sue's emotions. Then I decided to introduce a structure to explore and work with her defence.

THERAPIST: Let's concretise the message that forbids you to face your beloved sister and also your secret thoughts which you don't want your sister to know.

I supported Sue to set up a third chair for the secret thoughts. Sue needed to decide where to place this third chair, based on the current situation under exploration and her sense of the internal and interpersonal dynamic. Sue decided to put the chair beside her own chair.

THERAPIST: Role reverse with the secret thoughts. Secret thoughts, what do you say to Sue, what are your messages?

SUE AS SECRET THOUGHTS: I wish I could have replaced my sister in death, or at least died with her in the accident. However, don't tell my beloved sister as I don't want her to feel upset.

I recognised this as a key factor leading to Sue's suicidal ideations.

THERAPIST: Can you tell your sister those thoughts from your own role, Sue?

My hope here as the therapist was to support a direct encounter between Sue and her sister.

SUE: (shaking her head and remaining in the chair representing the role of her secret thoughts) I don't want my sister to know about me since I don't want her to feel worried and upset.

THERAPIST: Then tell your sister from this role, as secret thoughts, that are expressed in secret.

Here I tried to adapt the technique to facilitate the encounter while respecting Sue's need to continue to protect her sister from her feelings, even within the psychodramatic work.

SUE AS SECRET THOUGHTS: I love you so much. I wanted to die for you. You were the one bringing me to the hospital to see our father when he died. You were more useful, more valuable than me. Since I cannot die for you, I want to join you in death. I cannot bear the pain of losing anyone else in the family. I lost my beloved father and you, my sister. I prefer to die rather than have this pain again. It is too painful.

THERAPIST: Thank you, secret thoughts. Now return to your own chair in this encounter. Do you have any response to your secret thoughts, Sue? (Sue shakes her head)

OK, role reverse with your sister.

SUE: (in the role as her sister and with the support of therapist as double) I feel heartbroken and painful when I hear you saying that you want to die for me or to die with me. It is very silly for you to think that you can replace me in death. I went to America with my life aspiration. My death was caused by accident, and I had no control over it. It was my fate. Please don't think about dying for me or with me. I love you. I want you to have your own life and your future. I want you to have a good life and have your future. I bless you with my heart. I want you to live your life fully for yourself, and also for your love and honour to me.

THERAPIST: Reverse back. Respond to your sister.

Sue cried in silence. I stayed with her to support her, and gave her sufficient time and space to stay with her tears. It was a moment of catharsis, the emotional release from the long-repressed sadness of grief and loss.

THERAPIST: (aware of Sue's inability to speak, continuing to prompt as double, using the message Sue had given herself from her sister's role) "My heart feels pain. I want you to have your own life ... for your love and honour to me."

SUE: (crying) I hear very clearly what you say.

At this point, recognising her struggle to receive the positive messages given to herself when she was in her sister's role, I tried to help her consolidate those messages.

THERAPIST: Can you tell your sister how much you still love her and miss her?

SUE: (to sister) I love you very much, and I miss you.

THERAPIST: Can you tell your sister how much you treasure the birthday cards and gifts you received from her nearly 20 years ago?

SUE: I have kept the three birthday cards and small gifts you sent to me from America. I still keep all the cards in very good condition, and I take those cards out to look at them sometimes in memory of you.

THERAPIST: Role reverse with sister.

SUE AS HER SISTER: I sent those cards to you to tell you how much I love you and care about you.

THERAPIST: Reverse back.

SUE FROM HER OWN ROLE: I know you love me. You are the only one in the family I could share some of my feelings with, through writing letters to you when you were in America …

When the dialogue comes to an end, de-roling and debriefing are important. To de-role the client and space, I asked Sue to arrange the chairs back to the original space in the room as before the dialogue started. Both Sue and I went back to our original chairs, and we started to reflect on the session. Sue was invited to talk about her experience, and shared her sense of where we were regarding the relationship. Sue felt the session had provided her with the chance to tell her sister how much she had missed her in her life for so many years. Those tears she had held for many years were beginning to flow. At the beginning of the session, she could not allow herself to feel her emotions, as she was worried her feelings would go beyond death and make her sister upset today. She could begin to express her feelings in the role of her secret thoughts. She acknowledged how difficult it was for her to get in touch with her tears, having practised disconnecting from her feelings for so many years. She reflected that she dared not get in touch with her feelings at all in the past, and only with the support of the therapeutic relationship was she beginning to access the courage now to get in touch with her true feelings.

In this example, I have demonstrated how psychodrama was used to begin to move a stuck client on in the process of dealing with her unfinished business in grief and loss. Through the power of surplus reality and doubling, I was able to offer Sue the space to have a direct encounter with the sister she had lost and begin to express what had never been expressed before. It was an important step towards her resolving her issues. Role reversal helped her go beyond her restricted role, and to gain insight through engaging with the perspective of her sister. The exercise put her directly in touch with her belief that expressing her feelings damages the other, and so she was offered the additional role of her secret thoughts to allow her to express her deep and ambivalent feelings in grief. Sue got in touch with a feeling of shame regarding her suicidal ideations as she faced her sister in this encounter, and began to distance herself from her commitment to her wish to join her sister in death.

To support Sue to be conscious of her feelings and thoughts, and to express what has not been expressed, I used the double technique here. Much more than only reframing or reflection, it allowed me the chance to speak from the position of my client, with deeper attunement. The client has the full right to disown or modify any of the double's statements. Sue needed to frame my doubling statements in a way that was fitting for her.

In this session, her access to words was limited, and much of the process was conducted in silence on her part. Those words she did allow herself to say had all the more significance.

The work with her sister was about the more recent loss. The first traumatic loss in Sue's life was the sudden death of her father, which was the locus of her suicidal ideations. I offered the use of spectogram in combination with a timeline to support Sue to begin to address the earlier loss and to better understand the emergence and context of her suicidal ideations.

Use of spectogram

Spectogram, or the use of miniatures, helps the client to concretise things by placing objects or people into a symbolic arrangement with the aim of clarifying intra-psychic and interpersonal dynamics (Jennings, 1986, cited in Casson, 2007). I offered this technique to Sue to allow her to see the whole picture of her bereavements and her responses to them more clearly. As a technique, spectogram allows the use of role taking and encounter with a greater degree of aesthetic distance, which proved to be more manageable for her than the use of direct role work described above.

Timeline

I asked Sue to concretise the development of her suicidal ideation and its significance for her. I invited Sue to select different miniatures to represent different key moments in her life. The six moments she chose were: (1) the death of her father, symbolised by a stone staircase, which was relevant to the manner of his death; (2) witnessing her mother's suicidal responses to the death of her husband 22 years ago, symbolised by a black bat representing how haunting that memory is; (3) the death of her sister 18 years ago, symbolised by an owl that evoked the fact that it was night-time when the accident happened; (4) Sue missing the chance to go to America to attend her sister's funeral at that time, represented by an empty bucket evoking her sense of emptiness and loneliness; (5) Sue's current stressful life factors, symbolised by the hard shell of a tortoise. I also asked her to concretise her suicidal ideations in order to put the internal response outside, where it could be viewed in context. She chose a pillar box for this, evoking her sense of wanting to reconnect with those who have died at times of suicidal ideation. Sue placed the miniatures following the timeline perspective (Figure 9.1).

I invited her to encounter her father, mother, and her deceased sister through the small objects in front of us. Although this was far from easy for Sue, she managed to tell her father about her confusion as a 13-year-old facing his sudden death. How could he have left her in that way when she was his favourite and he the most important person in her life? This

Figure 9.1 Sue's timeline

question spoken on behalf of her younger bereaved self allowed her to access her tears. I invited her to reverse roles with her father internally and to respond from his role. From this role she was able to give her bereaved self (both the 13-year-old and her current self) a deeply reparative message. She found the words from his role to remind herself that she had her own life and to receive his blessing to live it. She went further and reminded herself that she could get good support from the people around her. At this point she turned to me and said that I was her angel sent by heaven to help her, following the sincere prayers of her father and sister in heaven. She was finding a way to integrate the significance of the therapy relationship into her own religious belief system.

We returned to this spectogram in a subsequent session, where Sue was able to consolidate the work she had been doing on her relationship with the second bereavement, the loss of her sister. From the role of her sister, with her finger on the symbol for her, she was able to reiterate the words of encouragement that we had worked so hard to find in her earlier sessions.

Finally, we moved on to an encounter with her mother. I invited her to add a symbol for mother into the spectogram. She chose a rabbit carrying food, and placed her into the sculpt. Sue was able to tell her how haunted she had been by her mother's words that she wanted to follow her husband, Sue's father, into death. This had conveyed to Sue the belief that suicide was an appropriate response to the loss of a loved one. Sue spoke of her fear of losing her mother, too, of being abandoned by both her parents at a moment when she particularly needed a mother, facing the shocking loss of her father. That was the moment she adopted the strategy of numbing herself to her own feelings, telling herself that this was how she could protect her mother from attempting suicide.

I asked her to attempt a role reversal with her mother, and repeated the essence of what Sue had expressed. From the role of her mother, she was able to acknowledge that the desire to die at that time of loss was very much an expression of how overwhelmed she had been with shock and grief, that it was never a serious plan or intention, that she had no idea how her words impacted her daughter, and that over the years she had managed to move on with her life, and wished the same for her daughter.

These psychodramatic encounters helped Sue put her life experience in context. It may be too strong a claim to say that she achieved closure. However, she acknowledged that the idea of escaping difficulties by attempting suicide had become a habit, not only in relation to loss, but also when facing the normal stresses of her work and domestic life in the present. This realisation opened the door towards a new phase of work in which she began to address these everyday stresses and take a step back from the extremity of her habitual suicidal responses.

Conclusion

A good therapeutic relationship is deemed paramount in our therapeutic work. According to Guntrip, the weak ego is in urgent need of a relationship, and the therapeutic relationship can fill the gap left by inadequate mothering (Guntrip, 1969, p. 231). Psychotherapy and reparative emotional experiences are desperately needed, but also very frightening for some clients for whom experiencing emotion is equated with being overwhelmed and unable to cope. As a psychotherapist, it is my job to provide a safe and holding environment for my clients, and to attempt to attune, to the best of my ability, especially where the work is of such a delicate nature.

The positive working alliance was crucial in this work, offering Sue a developmentally needed reparative experience to support her to find new role responses to life's developmental and existential crises. We found ways for the therapy to sit comfortably alongside the client's traditional belief system, and this enabled Sue to access and share her deeply painful emotions with me. She recognised our somewhat idealised relationship as reparative for her.

Although Sue sometimes struggled to fully engage with psychodrama as a method, by working slowly and patiently, it facilitated her to explore long-standing unfinished business. She gained perspective on the past, and by doing so was able to begin to question her responses to the present and engage in a more balanced way with the challenges of the future.

References

Casson, J. (2007). Psychodrama in miniature. In C. Baim, J. Burmeister, & M. Maciel (Eds), *Psychodrama: Advances in Theory and Practice*. Routledge.

Farmer, C. (1998). The psychodramatic treatment of depression. In M. Karp, P. Holmes, & K. Bradshaw-Kouvon (Eds), *The Handbook of Psychodrama*. Routledge.

Guntrip, H. (1969). *Schizoid Phenomena, Object Relations and the Self*. Marsfield Library.

Leick, N. & Davidsen-Nielsen, M. (1991). *Healing Pain*. Tavistock/Routledge.

Taylor, D. (2008). Psychoanalytic and psychodynamic therapies for depression: The evidence base. *Advances in Psychiatric Treatment*, 14(6), 401–413.

Chapter 10

Working psychodramatically with anxiety

Virginie Boury

Introduction

Anxiety can be a seriously debilitating condition. As Barlow writes: "Anxiety kills relatively few people, but many would welcome death as an alternative to the paralysis and suffering resulting from anxiety in its severe forms" (Barlow 2004, 18). In this chapter I begin by describing the physical and emotional state of anxiety from different theoretical perspectives. Then, through Oliver's case study, I show how I attempted to help him address this phenomenon within the context of one-to-one therapy in private practice. This work was informed by attachment theory which underpinned the use of psychodrama through which Oliver could explore his anxiety and develop a new transformative role in his life: the role of initiator.

Perspectives on anxiety

One in six people worldwide is afflicted with an anxiety disorder for at least a year during their lifetime, and this phenomenon extends far beyond the population diagnosed with anxiety disorder (Stossel 2013). In the UK, every week, one in six adults experiences a common mental health problem, such as anxiety or depression, and one in five adults has considered taking their own life at some point. Stossel groups the competing theories of and treatment approaches to anxiety into four categories: the biomedical, the cognitive-behavioural, the psychoanalytic and the experiential, and these often overlap.

From the biomedical perspective, we learn that when individuals experience anxiety, their amygdala is convinced that they are in danger and acts in order to protect them by making them ready for fight or flight in response to the perceived danger. The amygdala raises their blood sugar level to make sure that their muscles have a good level of energy to take action. It boosts their heart rate, and if this extra blood sent from the heart is not used by their muscles, it shows as flushing. As their heart rate climbs, the lungs have to work faster to make sure that the blood circulating in their body is supplied with enough oxygen. This phenomenon of flushing was very evident from my first contact with Oliver, and alerted me to the possibility that we would be working here with the theme of anxiety.

From a pharmacological perspective, anxiety is seen as a medical illness with dysfunctional biological mechanisms which can be rectified by medication. Selective serotonin reuptake inhibitors (SSRIs) are used to treat anxiety as they block the reuptake of serotonin in the synapses and therefore increase concentrations of serotonin in the amygdala that induce facilitation of serotonergic neurotransmission which decreases conditioned fear (Inoue et al. 2004).

Another theory and treatment approach is cognitive-behavioural therapy (CBT), which views anxiety as a conditioned fear response through which individuals come to fear objectively non-threatening things, or to fear objectively threatening things too intensively. So CBT treatment consists of correcting our thinking through various combinations of exposure therapy and cognitive restructuring. CBT considers anxiety as a philosophical problem caused by faulty thinking. According to Stossel, cutting-edge CBT borrows from the biomedical model, using pharmacology to enhance exposure therapy.

Oliver had previously engaged in CBT before approaching me. He reported that it gave him some helpful coping tools, but he felt that it did not lead to meaningful transformation in his life at an existential level.

The psychoanalytic approach holds that the repression of taboo thoughts or inner psychic conflicts lead to anxiety. So treatment involves bringing these repressed conflicts into conscious awareness and addressing them through psychodynamic psychotherapy in the pursuit of "insight". More specifically, object relations theory considers anxiety as a subjective experience motivated by some unconscious fear or conflict we carry in our internal world today from the past. From that perspective, anxiety is a state of turmoil, a state of helplessness which is a manifestation of something else that is repressed, such as abandonment, rage, anger, pain of loss, grief. According to the object relations view, anxiety masks feelings states which have been repressed or dissociated. Anxiety as a present phenomenon is a symptom of something unresolved from the past having been triggered. This perspective on the nature of anxiety was quite compatible with my experience of Oliver's process. As we explored his current life stressors and the manifestation of his anxiety in the present, all roads led to his early relationship with his mother.

Experiential approaches including psychodrama take an existential perspective and consider anxiety as a response to a perceived threat. Panic attacks and obsessional worrying are seen as coping mechanisms produced by the person in response to specific contexts which individuals experience as threats to their self-esteem or psychic integrity. Psychodrama focuses on the context and meaning of anxiety rather than only on the mechanisms of anxiety. We see anxiety as a somatic and psychological role response to existential and relational challenges that often have their origin in the past. We might support this work with the use of mindfulness exercises or guided relaxation to reduce symptoms.

According to Moreno, we are all cosmic beings connected to the universe and seeking to find our purpose and restore our soul and spirit, to become truly creative and spontaneous. The freedom of being creative and spontaneous can be frightening. From an existentialist point of view, the phenomenon of anxiety appears as individuals confront the possibility of freedom and feel the vertigo and dizziness of it. It is an ontological insecurity, the dread of annihilation, being overwhelmed and unable to cope, resulting in the disintegration of self, an emptiness, meaninglessness, nothingness or humiliation-mortification. When Oliver came to see me, he was filled with regret about the missed opportunities of living his creativity as a result of his paralysing anxiety.

Oliver and the development of the psychodramatic role of the initiator

Oliver was a 35-year-old single British man, a middle child with two brothers, also single, with whom he rarely had contact. He went to boarding school from the age of 11, where he felt homesick and often cried. Oliver described his mother as self-obsessed, lacking empathy, selfish and mean to him, but also full of energy and funny. He described his father as wise, unemotional and disengaged. It seemed that neither parent had been particularly well attuned to him as a child.

Oliver's professional work involved supervising a team of 15 people, which he found demanding and stressful.

Oliver referred himself to me to work on his social anxiety and panic attacks. He told me that he had attended CBT sessions in the past which had given him some practical tools, but left him ultimately dissatisfied. He was now ready for a therapy to explore more deeply what was driving his anxiety. He was searching for meaning.

I could hear his desperate need to be validated as someone struggling with anxiety, and witnessed in his difficulties within a containing relationship. He experienced himself as not fully alive, and wanted to move in a direction of reclaiming his life. He shared his isolation that was the consequence of his social anxiety, leaving him without an intimate relationship or meaningful friendships.

As a psychodrama psychotherapist in training, when I first encounter a client, I pay attention to the three dimensions of role: the somatic, the social and the psychological roles.

From the perspective of the somatic dimension of role, I noticed his fragility and vulnerability, conveyed by his way of holding his spine as he walked towards the chair. It was as if Oliver had no sense of being held by his spine. I might define this somatic role as a tentative, unsupported mover in the world.

He entered the space with a big smile on his face which seemed forced and incongruent. At the same time there were small, swift movements of the lips of which he seemed unconscious, and which evoked in me a feeling of anxiety. From the perspective of the social dimension of role, he clearly presented as shy, wanting to make a connection with me, while his way of approaching contact had the quality of false self about it, beyond the normal level of nervousness to be expected at a first meeting.

I noticed my own maternal countertransference, as if I were encountering a little boy girding his loins to face the daunting task of entering the play-ground. This led me to wonder if I had met his psychodramatic role of the brave little soldier or the abandoned child putting on a brave face.

In addition to my maternal countertransference, I was aware of a positive tele, the Morenian term for the "inter-personal chemistry ... the simplest unit of feeling transmitted from one individual towards another" (Moreno 1953, 314). I liked him, found him *sympathique* and had a sense that he had warmed to me.

Following the role analytic model from the London Centre for Psycho-drama, I was trying to formulate a role analysis for each session's content and to identify which underdeveloped roles Oliver needed to own more and develop in his life. My approach was to direct Oliver to explore his feeling states and belief systems behind the anxiety, thus revealing his internal working model learnt and encoded from the past.

This exploration started by concretising Oliver's anxiety, bringing it alive in the therapeutic space and developing the encounter through role reversal. Oliver chose a crow sounder (a constant, obsessive noise) from the musical instruments. Standing up close to it, I asked Oliver to be this anxiety, the crow sounder, and speak from this role to Oliver.

Anxiety's message to Oliver was:

> I am always there, I stop you from enjoying life, I stop you from being happy, I make you think all the time and ruminate, I make you have frightening thoughts, I prevent you from connecting with others, having fun, being spontaneous. I am always there with you.

This first step into psychodramatic exploration brought relief as it helped Oliver to relate to his anxiety rather than being it. From his own role, he expressed his feeling of exhaustion and a desire to do something about it: "You make me miserable and lonely, and I am sick and tired of it. Where do you come from?" In some way, this was the beginning of Oliver's search for the underdeveloped role of the initiator. At the same time, there was a sense of despair and a belief that this was beyond his capacity.

Oliver brought into the sessions recent and less recent situations where he experienced overwhelming anxiety, some of those including panic attacks. These situations included walking past a stranger in the street and believing the other person was looking at him and judging him, being at a restaurant with old school friends and being unable to join the conversation, and doing a presentation at work where he managed to deliver the presentation, but with great personal effort and bathed in sweat. I invited him to bring each of these scenarios into the space. This enabled him to show me his experience of what had happened there and then and reflect on it with me in the here and now. In terms of *context*, we could see that his anxiety was active in public places, in social situations and under the spotlight at work – in fact, in most situations where Oliver was in the presence of others, whether known or unknown. His *behaviour*, in term of his somatic roles, included sweating, a tightening of the throat and difficulty breathing. Socially, he was very watchful of others, obsessing about how others relate to each other and wondering how they perceive him, while isolating himself, withdrawing and going silent, blocking himself from taking any initiative to connect. In terms of the psychological role, his impulse was to become the invisible man, to dissociate. His *feeling* response was anxiety, panic, a sense of loneliness, sadness and emptiness. The *beliefs* driving this role response were: I am alone and unable to connect; I am stupid and uninteresting; I will never be able to relate on an emotional level; if I don't keep observing other people I will disappear, the only way to stay anchored in the present is to keep thinking about the others; I am an empty soul and people see through me. The *consequences* for him were an almost total lack of spontaneity and creativity, chronic anxiety and an existential state of extreme isolation.

In this first phase of the therapy we identified the overdeveloped roles of the anxious, self-critical man, the obsessive observing thinker. It also helped us to formulate a more specific aim for our therapeutic work together, namely to work on his underdeveloped role of spontaneous initiator. Oliver could see that if he developed his capacity to spontaneously initiate action, he would be able to introduce change into his lonely life and meet others, including a potential partner.

Hence, in the second phase of the work, the aim was to track back the beliefs identified above, to explore how they came into being. Much of this work involved locus scenes where his mother was present.

As the work progressed, Oliver brought his anxiety into the session less and less. He increasingly expressed his readiness to explore internal and external dynamics when in relationship with his mother and brought scenes from the past where she was there.

By revisiting numerous scenes from his childhood, Oliver realised and showed me how as a boy his emotional needs were met by a lack of attunement and an overwhelming chaotic response from his mother. He learnt that expressing his needs and emotions would risk damaging her. She was clearly highly anxious, and would scream and shout when he became emotional. It was a matter of survival for him to maintain his attachment to his mother by constantly thinking about her. This was how he could create a sense of emotional containment. He became his mother's protector whose mission was to be constantly preoccupied by her so as to understand her internal world. Through his constant preoccupation with his mother's needs, he became her carer at the expense of his own experience of childhood. These scenes from the past demonstrated how his attachment strategy first developed. As Baim (2014) writes, the attachment strategy first develops to protect the self from dangers, real or perceived, in relation to the attachment figure(s). Through psychodramatic exploration, Oliver came to see how his overdeveloped observer role helped him survive the unpredictability of his mother and her lack of attunement. In one psychodramatic scene from his teenage years, he represented his mother engaged in conversation with his older brother while ignoring him, Oliver. From the role of his teenage self, Oliver shared: "I need to keep thinking about her in order to understand her, to believe that somehow she does care for me, to find a meaning to her meanness to me."

Vignette: Oliver's sense of isolation and inability to connect with others

This is one of a number of scenes through which we explored the origin of Oliver's belief that he is alone in the world and unable to connect to others. The memory that he brought onto the psychodramatic stage was an incident that took place when he was eight years old. His godmother was visiting and his father was absent. Oliver was uneasy around his godmother and did not like her continual intrusive questioning of him. He made an excuse to his mother that he was feeling sick, and went up to his bedroom and put himself to bed. As he enacted this conversation with his mother through the use of role reversal, it emerged that his intention was to communicate his emotional state to his mother through the language of somatisation. His wish was that she would understand the subtext: "Please see me, understand me, sympathise with me and soothe me, and help me manage this." In fact, her response was to let him go upstairs alone while she continued her conversation with his godmother for some time. As he laid in bed, he heard their voices chatting to each other. After a period of time, his mother came up to see him briefly to check on him, apparently to assuage her own anxiety. He was longing for some tender words and attention, to know that she was curious about him and concerned. Instead, the exchange was short and devoid of any attunement or physical contact. When she left the room to return to her friend, Oliver felt alone and told himself that he was responsible for the failure in connection. If his mother couldn't see him, he was clearly invisible and unable to connect with the other. He remained in the bedroom, passive, isolated and inert.

Stepping outside of the scene and viewing it from mirror, Oliver was able to make a connection with his younger self and remembered how for many years as a child the same image kept popping into his head: two eggs close to each other, one whole, the other covered in small cracks. We discussed the meaning of this image to him in relation to the scene in front of us. Concretely, there was a representation of his childhood bedroom on the stage in front of us, pieces of fabric to represent the bed and the bedroom door. In his mind's eye, however, Oliver could see his younger self in the scene and used the recurrent metaphor of the two eggs to make sense of what he saw. The whole egg represented Oliver's desperate desire to be held and contained. The cracked one represented his image of himself as fundamentally flawed: "As I look at this little boy, I recognise that I've always believed that I am weird, that I was made wrong, there was something wrong in me." Oliver's image put me in touch with Balint's concept of the basic fault, which describes that something was wrong or missing within "the mother-infant unit (a dual unit)" (Balint 1949, 99). Through the discrepancy he experienced with his mother, Oliver came to strongly believe that the lack of fit between himself and the people around him was his fault.

As we reflected on this piece of work, Oliver was able to link his habitual anxiety in his current life with his need as a child to constantly wonder about his mother's mind and her behaviour towards him. He illustrated this by slipping into role as his younger self and sharing his internal monologue:

> Why is she mean to me, is she going to shout, why is she curious about my brothers and ignores me, what have I done wrong? Keep wondering, stay alert, keep thinking about her, that is the only way to stay connected to her.

From an early age, anxiety was the best strategy Oliver could create at that time in response to the unpredictably responsive mother. The mission of his anxiety was to help him fill an internal empty space and maintain some attachment to his primary parental figure despite her absence of attunement, her chaotic and inconsistent care, her total lack of curiosity about him.

Reparative moments: the birth of the initiator role

Throughout our work I invited Oliver to look at what he had created on the psychodramatic stage from the mirror position, as described above. From there I gave some time to Oliver to listen internally to the messages

Working psychodramatically with anxiety 137

he had spoken out from the roles brought into the specific scene in front of us. I then asked Oliver how he felt witnessing those dynamics, and what changes needed to happen. I noticed an interesting development in Oliver in response to my questions from mirror. At first he would respond by describing and analysing. These comments came from his highly developed observer role. Over time, Oliver began quite spontaneously to actively address his comments both to himself and his mother on the stage. We marked this shift as the birth of his initiator role. An example follows.

Oliver to his younger self:

> You are very sad and anxious because it is impossible to make sense of her meanness. You tell yourself it's your own fault but it isn't. It is not your fault and despite the way you get treated I can see your spark, your aliveness and creativity. I want to connect more with that spark in my life today. Don't let your emotions run dry. You are not at fault, she just has too many problems and it is not up to you to save her. She is not able to contain what you are going through because she is not able to understand herself.

Oliver to his mother:

> All your shouting and meanness to him makes him confused, sad and anxious. You made him believe that it is his fault. All my life, I have been watching and trying to understand. I don't want to keep being so watchful and trying to second guess your moods. I know you are depressed and anxious but that's not my responsibility.

This development within the therapy space of Oliver's capacity to allow spontaneous responses to the scenes we were exploring was very empowering for Oliver. Breaking through to his capacity to initiate and challenge helped Olivier develop self-belief to initiate change. In parallel, Oliver would increasingly report instances from his life outside the therapy space where he was practising this new role, being active and making changes in his life without too big an impact from his anxiety. As his initiator role grew, his anxiety receded.

Towards closure

Towards the end of our work together, as he entered the space with a genuine big smile on his face and a haircut, looking grounded and open, Oliver said: "I have decided to take a sabbatical, to live a life which makes me ready to meet somebody, I feel my *joie de vivre* again."

When I heard Oliver using a French expression, it sounded to me like a wish to create a spontaneous complicity with me as a French person and that it was an expression of gratitude in preparation of our work ending. I offered him an opportunity to create an image to concretise his *joie de vivre*. Oliver created a sculpt from the following different objects: a black and white photograph representing a baby sitting in a bucket full of water, laughing out loud, spontaneous and alive, a small sailing boat symbolising his ability to respond to and catch opportunities as they come. He then told me he was enjoying meditation and long walks in nature, and picked up a red leaf to represent his ability to nurture himself in this way.

To complete his sculpt, Oliver wanted an object that symbolised his desire to connect. He hesitated, felt anxious, but then chose a black and white photograph representing a group of people moving together (Figure 10.1).

We discussed the sculpt and its meaning for Oliver.

The laughing baby in a bath reminded him how safe he felt in the therapy, and of his new connection to the child within. The image had a message of love, care and attunement. The positive therapeutic alliance had provided an important counterpoint to the painful work of revisiting his early attachment issues and their link with his anxiety.

Looking at his sculpt, Oliver said with a genuine smile on his face:

> I learnt a lot from the work I have been doing here, I trusted you. By being in my mother's shoes, I understood her but I cannot change her,

Figure 10.1 Oliver's sculpt

I might help her sometimes but I need to take care of myself. I feel ready to meet somebody.

In our last session, as we reflected on the reality of separation and closure, I asked Oliver to choose an object to symbolise his ability to rebound when feeling overwhelmed and no longer having the therapy space as an external resource. Oliver chose a statue of Ganesh, the Hindu God, and said: "I don't want to sink into depression, I have been there too long. This represents my creativity and spirituality." Ganesh is seen as the lord of success and the destroyer of evils and obstacles. His elephantine head represents wisdom, and the trunk symbolises Om, the sound of cosmic reality. What a long way we had come from the harsh squawking of the crow sounder. Some weeks later, Oliver announced that he had decided to take a sabbatical to India. I regarded this as strong evidence of his commitment to the developing role of initiator. Oliver actively brought this new role into being, and with it his faith in his *joie de vivre*.

Conclusion

In this chapter I have described the physical and emotional state of anxiety from different perspectives. I have introduced my one-to-one client Oliver, who was able to explore his anxiety on the psychodramatic stage in his sessions with me. Through the use of role analysis we were able to make meaning from Oliver's memories and link these to the development of his anxiety, a role which had become entrenched and was seriously limiting his current life experience. Through accessing his spontaneity on the psychodrama stage, Oliver developed a counterbalance to the role of anxiety, in the form of a new role: that of the initiator. A key moment in this process was his psychodramatic encounter with his child self in the presence of his dismissive, preoccupied mother. The whole therapy was a transformative process for Oliver, but in retrospect, I am aware that I may have colluded with him, and probably with his family as well, in not bringing father onto the stage in order to explore his part in the development of Oliver's anxiety. Nonetheless, the therapy was "good enough" to enable him to initiate changes in his current life.

References

Baim, C. (2014). Integrating psychodrama with attachment theory: Implications. In P. Holmes, M. Farrall and K. Kirk (eds). *Empowering Therapeutic Practice*. London: Jessica Kingsley

Balint, M. (1949). Early developmental states of the ego: Primary object love. *International Journal of Psychoanalysis* 30: 265–273.

Barlow, D. H. (2004). *Anxiety and Its Disorders*. London: Guildford Press.

Inoue, T. Li, X. B. Abekawa, T., Kitaichi, Y., Izumi, T., Nakagawa, S., Koyama, T. (2004). Selective serotonin reuptake inhibitor reduces conditioned fear through its effect in the amygdala. *European Journal of Pharmacology* 497 (3): 311–316.

Moreno, J. L. (1953) *Who Shall Survive?* Beacon, NY: Beacon House.

Stossel, S. (2013). *My Age of Anxiety.* New York: Alfred A. Knopf.

Chapter 11

One-to-one psychodrama with eating disorders

Eva Koumpli

Introduction

In this chapter, I aim to provide an overview of how I apply psychodrama in individual psychotherapy in order to help sufferers of eating disorders heal from their underlying trauma(s), make tangible changes and find a new way of being in the world, free from their eating disorder. My aim as a clinician is to address the whole person, not only the symptom, in order to facilitate transformation and post-traumatic growth. Taking into consideration the neuroscience that supports our understanding of eating disorders and trauma, I foster a holistic approach that is based on psychodramatic methodology, role theory, and elements of other creative therapies and body-based approaches. Working with eating disorders requires a team of professionals that oversee the physical and mental well-being of the sufferer. This includes a psychotherapist, a nutritional therapist, a specialist doctor and in some situations a psychiatrist.

The chapter begins with research that shows the correlation between trauma and eating disorders, and it continues with theoretical underpinnings from neuroscience and psychodrama theory. A case study demonstrates how I applied psychodrama and role analysis in one-to-one therapy with a female sufferer of diabulimia. I have focused on key moments and turning points.

Understanding eating disorders

Suffering from an eating disorder is a daunting and secretive experience characterised by perpetual and pervasive feelings of dread and shame. Research has shown that there is a correlation between eating disorders and trauma (Brewerton, 2007; Briere and Scott, 2007). A sufferer's distorted relationship with food is only the symptom of trauma(s) that has resulted in them having low self-worth and poor body image, using self-destructive ways to cope with painful feelings, making choices based on fear, striving for perfection, having the need for a false sense of control in their life and sabotaging any form of intimacy in relationships. Being in a relationship authentically, without masks or pretences, can be a very threatening experience for a sufferer, whose disordered relationship with food and their body will gradually supersede all other relationships.

Other studies (O'Shaughnessy and Dallos, 2009;Zachrisson and Skårderud, 2010;Tasca and Balfour, 2014) suggest that there is a relation between eating disorders and attachment issues. Most of our beliefs about ourselves, others and the world are born in our most significant early relationships. The eating disorder primarily serves as a coping mechanism that ensures that past wounds on these intimate issues are not remembered or repeated in the present. In *Why She Feels Fat*, Johanna McShane and Tony Paulson write to the families and carers of those suffering with an eating disorder:

> Eating disorders are powerful coping mechanisms that help an individual manage the parts of life that feel too much to bear. [Your loved one] ... experiences her eating disorder as a source of support even though its symptoms are, in reality, harmful to her. Your loved one doesn't feel threatened by it. On the contrary, she feels threatened without it.
>
> (McShane and Paulson, 2008, in Shapiro, 2009, p. 110)

The idealisation of thinness by our culture and the media plays an enormous role in the increase of eating disorders. It is estimated that 85% of American women diet chronically and 75% are ashamed of their body size and shape (Bloom et al., 1994). In the UK, women's body dissatisfaction is a theme that has attracted interest for surveys in very popular magazines. A survey conducted by *Glamour* magazine in 2011 showed that 97% of women admitted to having at least one "I hate my body" moment a day, with an average of 13 negative body thoughts every day. As a result of such cultural influence, puberty is often a time during which girls begin to develop eating disorders. Learnt experiences and trauma, along with a society that glorifies thinness, restrictive eating and avoids vulnerability, create the perfect foundation for the onset of an eating disorder. Becoming a woman, having curves and gaining weight – experiences that are a necessary part of this developmental stage – become shameful and embarrassing.

However, body image issues and eating disorders are definitely not gender-specific, particularly with the rising numbers of male eating disorders and body dysmorphic disorders. There is a growing pressure for men to be thinner, stronger, muscular and meet the standards of an idealised masculine body. The Centre for Appearance Research at the University of the West of England found after interviewing 384 British men that 35% would trade a year of their life to achieve the ideal body and shape. The most widely quoted study estimates that males have a lifetime prevalence of 0.3% for anorexia nervosa (AN), 0.5% for bulimia nervosa (BN) and 2% for binge eating disorder (BED). These figures correspond to males representing 25% of individuals with AN and BN and 36% of those with BED.

Neuroscience and trauma: the body remembers what the mind forgets

Trauma expert Bessel Van der Kolk suggests that experiential therapy that engages trauma survivors holistically should be the therapy of choice for trauma, and he values the therapeutic qualities of theatre and improvisation (Van der Kolk, 2014). Sufferers of trauma find it hard to use words to describe their internal experiences because Broca's area, one of the speech centres in the left brain, is de-activated as a result of trauma. Without a functioning Broca's area, we cannot put our thoughts and feelings into words. The limbic system, our emotional control centre, controls the hypothalamus, and under stress it sounds an alarm that stimulates the hypothalamus to release cortico-releasing hormone (CRH). CRH stimulates the pituitary gland to release adrenocortico-tropic hormone (ACTH). The sympathetic system responds by releasing epinephrine and norepinephrine, which increase blood flow, heart rate and respiration to protect us from danger, producing a flight or fight response. In response to ACTH, the adrenal glands release cortisol, which informs the limbic system when the danger is over. Then the alarm is off, and the body returns to balance. Under chromic stress, the ongoing release of cortisol exhausts the adrenal glands, which increase reliance on stimulants like sugar and coffee. The brain's amygdala, which helps us store and process our emotions, is hyperaroused, which results in experiencing intense feelings followed by dissociation.

As Van Der Kolk states

> if we want to change post-traumatic reactions, we have to access the emotional brain and do "limbic system therapy": repairing faulty alarms systems and restoring the emotional brain to its ordinary job of being a quiet background presence that takes care of the housekeeping of the body, ensuring that you eat, sleep, connect with intimate partners, protect your children, and defend against danger.
>
> (Van der Kolk, 2014, p. 203)

Role theory

Morenian role theory is a central concept in my work with eating disorders, which provides a way of exploring the meaning of an eating disorder in a sufferer's life and the sufferer's way of being in relation to self, others and the wider world. According to Moreno, role is the functioning form the individual takes in any moment (Moreno, 1961). The sense of self emerges as the individual takes on roles in relation to others and to their

144 Eva Koumpli

environment (Moreno, 1953). Moreno's role theory involves three categories of roles: somatic, social and psychodramatic.

Somatic roles

These are physical roles: for example, eater, sleeper, dancer. We are embodied organisms, breathing, moving, eating, digesting and sleeping. Somatic roles are usually dysfunctional in sufferers of eating disorders, hence they constitute a central focus in therapy. Sufferers of eating disorders have a poor and distorted relationship with their bodies, their mind and body are disconnected, and their awareness of their senses and sensations is very fragmented. The goal in therapy is to gain awareness of their body, senses, sensations, posture and breath, which leads to an understanding of their feelings and hunger signals, the ability to feel present and grounded, and to self-reflect and self-soothe.

From a nutritional perspective, a central somatic role that needs to be developed is that of the intuitive eater. Intuitive eating means knowing how to respond appropriately to our hunger, eating when we need to eat, and stopping when we are satisfied. We are all born knowing how to eat intuitively. Just think of a newborn that cries when it needs feeding and turns away when it feels full. Without these innate internal signals of hunger and satiety, we would not survive as a species. Authors of *Intuitive Eating* Tribole and Resch (1995) refer to this process as "a journey back to intuitive eating", as you are not learning anything new, just reconnecting with the power that you have always had to listen to your body.

Social roles

Social roles define our relationships, whether within the family (brother, sister, daughter, uncle), within the workplace (chief executive, personal assistant, cook, cleaner, teacher, actor) or in our social life (lover, mate, club secretary, group member, resident). In Morenian terms, it is important to describe the relationship with an adjective and a noun (e.g. a hurt daughter). The description of the role brings with it a narrative. It is how we experience ourselves and act in these relationships at any moment that expresses who we are.

In the treatment of eating disorders, exploration of well-developed and underdeveloped social roles is of paramount importance, as it helps the sufferer identify and reflect on the costs and consequences of their eating disorder, its effect on relationships and potential opportunities lost, the role of their eating disorder in their life, and the relationships that enable their eating disorder. The role of the eating disorder is context-specific, and exploration of the sufferer's social roles can help them identify repeated patterns of behaviour and the context within which their eating disorder behaviours emerge.

Psychodramatic roles

Psychodramatic roles, sometimes referred to as psychological roles, are the roles that are played out in our fantasy and imagination. In the treatment of eating disorders, exploration of these roles takes us into the inner world of the individual, the roles that they have internalised, their fulfilled and unfulfilled wishes. In terms of resourcing, as we move towards trauma work, this process can help a client identify and re-connect with nurturing and protective figures, or heroes from books/movies that have inspired them. Psychodramatic roles can also include role models.

Role analysis

I follow the role analysis taught by Jinnie Jefferies (1998), which consists of a methodical approach whereby roles are explored based on the following five factors:

1. the context in which they arise;
2. the behaviours;
3. the feelings in response to a given context;
4. the core beliefs that have been sedimented within an individual about self, others and the wider world, and which drive a behavioural response or reaction; tracking the belief system methodically leads to a safe and meaningful exploration of trauma which is the root cause of the role of the eating disorder;
5. the consequences of the pattern.

Role analysis helps me to formulate a treatment plan and strategy that enable the sufferer to methodically explore their self-construct, their worldview and the underlying reasons for their eating disorder. Role analysis is formed over time, and it enhances my collaborative work with the nutritional therapist. My role analysis often helps the nutritional therapist gain a deeper and more thorough understanding of the triggers and eating patterns of the client, and the feedback of the nutritional therapist helps me elaborate on my role analysis and the areas of focus at different stages of therapy.

Sufferers of eating disorders have complex internal worlds, and their need for control characterises their relationships with significant others. This is inevitably reflected in the therapeutic alliance, particularly in psychodrama, a relationship therapy that challenges a participant on bodily, cognitive and emotional levels. I consider the quality of encounter to be a very important value to seek to maintain towards my clients, so that the therapeutic relationship eventually becomes more important for the sufferer than their relationship with their eating disorder. The quality of the encounter precedes the technique, for it allows a safe environment within

146   Eva Koumpli

which a trusting relationship can develop, which is often unique and unlike any other previous relationships, and can help a sufferer delve into deeply ingrained and sedimented core beliefs, values and patterns of behaviour that comprise their current self-construct.

Susanne's journey

Susanne was a 22-year-old woman suffering from diabulimia. Diabulimia is an eating disorder in which people with Type 1 diabetes deliberately give themselves less insulin than they need for the purpose of weight loss. When insulin is omitted, calories are purged through the loss of glucose in the urine. Individuals with diabulimia manipulate insulin to prevent weight gain. According to DSM-5, this is one of the criteria of bulimia nervosa. Although diabulimia is not yet a recognised medical term, cases of Type 1 diabetes combined with eating disorders have been published since the 1980s (Hillar, Lobo, and Keeling, 1983; Hudson, Wentworth, and Hudson, 1983).

Susanne was diagnosed with Type 1 diabetes when she was 13 years old. She was diagnosed with diabulimia at the age of 21, but she had started manipulating her insulin intake long before the diagnosis. Susanne had attended a residential treatment programme prior to commencing therapy with me. She was a law graduate, and after completing her residential treatment, she started a master's degree. She found it really hard to concentrate on her studies, her mental and physical well-being were deteriorating, and her relationships were so affected that she had begun to isolate. So she decided to defer from university to focus on her recovery. While working with me, she was receiving nutritional therapy and she was attending an eating disorders support group. Her physical health was monitored by her endocrinologist and GP.

The eating disorder versus the well voice

From what I have observed phenomenologically in myself and others in therapeutic and non-therapeutic instances, when we wish to stop or change some recurring life patterns, there is very often a part of ourselves that desires the opposite, usually what is the most familiar, even if it is destructive or self-harming. This divided stance and the conflict between its opposing desires, when it is not reflected on, usually maintains the repeated patterns and keeps us stuck where we are. By raising our consciousness of our conflicting desires, we are in a better place to confront our behaviours, sedimented core beliefs and values more adequately. I have found that clients who have an eating disorder (ED) benefit enormously from having a safe space where they can become more aware of the internal dialogue between their two conflicting roles – their eating disorder and their wellness – for it enables them to explore their experience of being in the world with an eating disorder, so that eventually the attitudes, sedimented beliefs and dissociations that maintain the role of their eating disorder in their lives, become more explicit, conscious and eventually challengeable.

Susanne's process of exploring her internal dialogue between her eating disorder and her well voice was a crucial aspect of her therapeutic journey that laid the foundation for a deeper exploration of her self-construct. An encounter with her ED voice and well voice through the use of empty chairs led to a significant exploration of her meaning-world, and the role of her eating disorder as a necessary component of that meaning-world. This exploration involved Susanne role reversing with her ED voice and her well voice. Some key messages of the role of her ED were: "I'm protecting you ... without me you will be fat and everybody will reject you," "Without me, you cannot cope with your feelings," "You need me ... everybody has let you down, but I'm still here," "Without me you are not in control," "If you leave me, you will put weight on and nobody will like you ... without me you are fat and disgusting," "Without me everybody will see how boring you are and nobody will be interested in you." The messages of the role of the well voice were: "You are beautiful," "You are enough," "Your ED does not protect you ... if you don't take your insulin, you will die," "You deserve to eat, you deserve to be loved," "Your ED keeps you isolated, it doesn't protect you at all," "Don't be afraid of your feelings ... your feelings will not kill you, your ED will kill you."

An important part of this exploration was also a direct dialogue between the two voices, where Susanne had the opportunity to experientially explore her conflicting voices, the intensity of her ED, and practise challenging it from the role of the well voice. This exploration provided Susanne with the opportunity to rehearse in the session a way of not accepting passively the messages of her ED, but challenging them by embodying and expanding the role of her well voice. Engaging in that internal dialogue and challenging the ED voice is something that Susanne was encouraged to continue doing in between the sessions when she was in situations where her ED was strong. Journaling was a very important component of this process, as it helped Susanne to elaborate on her internal dialogue and release and contain some overwhelming feelings and thoughts between the sessions.

As the work progressed, Susanne began to explore the context within which the role of her ED was emerging. In a session after a binge-purge episode, we dramatised her experience by using scene setting. The situation took place at a party, where a lot of her peers from university were. I asked Susanne to use objects that represented those peers that were significant and also anything that was important in order to have the essence of the atmosphere of the party. She concretised with objects the four people (two male, two female) that she spent most of the evening with, the buffet and a guy that was flirting with her (they did not know each other prior to the party). Then I asked Susanne to introduce the four people she was with by role reversing with them. They all knew each other from their undergraduate studies, and all of them (apart from Susanne, who had deferred from her post-graduate studies) were continuing their studies in high-calibre universities. Only one of them (Susanne's female best friend) knew that Susanne had deferred from university due to her ED. The rest of them believed that she had deferred because she wanted to go travelling. Their conversation was mainly focused on catching up since they last saw each other and on "small talk", as Susanne said. We explored Susanne's internal and external messages. Externally, she was pretending that she was having fun, and she had prepared a story to say about "her travelling" and her plans to go back to university next year. Internally, she was very anxious, ashamed and self-critical about how she was perceived by the others. Some key messages of her critical voice in soliloquy were: "I'm fat," "Everybody has noticed that I have put weight on," "They all think that I'm boring and stupid," "I'm worthless ... I can't even commit to my studies," "I don't have anything to contribute to the conversation," "I shouldn't have come to this party," "They (friends) are pretending that they are having a good time with me, but they are bored." Role reversing with her friends, we explored what she perceived to be unspoken. Their messages in soliloquy were: "Susanne is a failure ... she is stupid ... ugly ... fat ... boring." Only her best friend (who knew about Susanne's ED) was more compassionate. In the role of the friend who knew about Susanne's ED, she expressed rejecting thoughts: "Susanne is so ill. She is not as interesting as she used to be. She always seems to have all these health issues. I'm not sure if I enjoy being her friend any more." Susanne felt ashamed, and when someone that was drunk was flirting with her, she became increasingly anxious. She was fearful that she would lose control and do something that she would regret afterwards. She felt anxious about choosing what to eat from the buffet. Role reversing with the buffet, she described it in the following way:

> I'm a buffet full of disgusting and fatty food ... desserts, carbs, cheese ... I offer such a variety of foods, but none of them is going to be healthy. If you eat any of these, you will not be able to stop and you will put weight on. Stay away.

Susanne avoids eating in front of others, but she is drinking a lot of alcohol in order to feel more confident and numb her feelings. She leaves the party, and on her way home she has a massive binge. Then she feels ashamed and angry at herself for losing control and binging, and as a result, the following day she omits her insulin in order to gain control and lose weight. After that, she feels even more ashamed and angry at herself for not being self-caring and losing control.

One-to-one psychodrama with eating disorders 149

In the mirror position, Susanne saw the situation, her feelings and thoughts more objectively without judging them. This is consistent with the practice of mindfulness and its concept of being present to emotions without judging them. Susanne was able to see the situation from some distance and make some links between her feelings, thoughts and behaviours. This led to her beginning to have more compassion towards herself:

> Don't be harsh on yourself. You are so overwhelmed and you need to take care of yourself. Your health is more important than university. When you are well, you can go back to your studies. You are enough, you are not a failure. Fighting an ED is so courageous. There's not any evidence that they (friends) think all these things about you. Why would they be here with you if they didn't like you?

We named this role "the Compassionate Self". A very important message that she gave from that role was: "You deserve to eat. You have been starving for so many days." This was a moment of insight, as it became apparent to Susanne that the binge was the result of a period of restriction. Susanne was restricting and fasting for days prior to the party as a result of her anxiety about being seen as fat. So her eating pattern was: restrictive eating–binging–omitting insulin. Up to that point, Susanne had seen herself only as a compulsive binge eater, and she was not aware of the restrictive pattern of her eating cycle.

On reflection, Susanne elaborated on how worthless she felt without her academic identity, and she explained that her punitive and self-loathing attitude were a result of her inability to be perfect. She also became more aware of the paradox that her ED behaviours were life-threatening, yet they were her only self-affirming behaviours in response to the rejecting and unloving stance of her world. Sharing her inner world and shame with me (a representative of the "others" in her world) offered her significant relief. There was something deeply transformational in exposing her shame and being met with empathy.

I made a role analysis on the basis of what we had explored in the session, as follows:

Context: In a social situation where she socialises with significant others (peers)

Behaviours: She restricts prior to the party, she hides her true feelings/thoughts and pretends that she is having a good time, she avoids eating in front of others, she is thinking self-conscious thoughts and obsessing about what other are thinking and not saying explicitly about her. She excessively drinks alcohol in order to feel more confident and cope with her feelings, she leaves the party and on her way home, when she is on her own, she binges. Then she purges by omitting insulin.

Beliefs: She believes that she is "fat ... stupid ... boring ... worthless ... a failure" and that others see her in this way, but they do not say it explicitly. She thinks that she shouldn't have gone to the party and that all foods at the party are her enemies; if she eats, she will put weight on. She also believes that she has nothing to contribute to the conversations and that without her academic identity, she is worthless. She believes that her illness provokes rejecting thoughts in her best friend.

Feelings: She feels ashamed, anxious, afraid of losing control.

Consequences: She isolates herself and she ends up feeling even worse. She puts her health and life at risk by omitting her insulin.

Her reflections on her ED cycle and her insights were followed up in her nutritional therapy, and she explored ways of being proactive when she knew that she would be in similar situations that fuel her ED or when she had to apply food challenges in a social context (e.g. she used the affirmation "I am enough" as a mantra in preparation for situations that would provoke her belief "I'm not perfect, I should be doing better"). The role of her Compassionate Self was also a role that she practised and nurtured outside the sessions in social situations.

Connecting with the body

Before moving on to working with trauma, we have to make sure that clients have reached a place where they can make sense of their feelings and they can self-regulate. Helping them to connect with their body is a very important part of this process. Clients with eating disorders speak a language about their body that we must help them to understand and decode. Psychic distress is located in the body, so when Susanne feels out of control because she is not perfect or she is frightened of being rejected, she looks in the mirror and sees herself as fat, or she says that she "feels fat", and she believes that fatness is the cause of her distress. She then focuses on changing and controlling her body. In her desperate attempt to seek a sense of control, she focuses on something concrete (her body) which she could effectively control. She was unable to see the connection between her mind and her body. Helping clients make sense of the language of their bodies requires paying attention to our somatic responses as therapists as well as helping the clients pay attention to theirs.

My sessions with Susanne incorporated mindfulness, safe space meditations and visualisations that helped her to begin the process of connecting with her body and finding a safe space within herself. As part of this process, we also focused our exploration on helping her to identify where in her body she experiences different feelings. I asked Susanne to draw an outline of her body. I asked her to close her eyes and recall a situation that she was feeling angry about. Then I asked her to notice her bodily sensations connected to the feeling of anger, shifting her attention between the situation and her body. We followed the same exploration for all primary feelings (Hendricks and Hendricks, 1993, Hudgins and Toscani, 2013, p. 227). Her tentative discovery that her body was not as alien as she thought proved to be a turning point in her recovery, for it helped her to identify feelings that she had previously disowned and it provided her with an emotional language that she had been lacking up to that point.

A next step was to help Susanne to cultivate her body empathy in order to make sense of her need to control her body and her hunger signs, and also identify what her body needs so that she could become more self-caring and take responsibility for her insulin intake. As we were moving towards a closer therapeutic alliance, I found myself holding in my body a very strong bodily counter-transference in the sessions. I often experienced the same bodily sensations as her or I held in my body the feelings that she was not able to identify at times. I was becoming increasingly aware that Susanne was experiencing a maternal transference towards me, and I was mindful not to slip into a place of enmeshment with her, which is exactly what her relationship with her mother looked like. Susanne's mum was very controlling, and Susanne was becoming more and more aware of how enmeshed their relationship was. She used to say at the beginning of her therapeutic journey that her mum was her best friend. Later on, it became quite apparent to Susanne that her mum was enabling her eating disorder by treating her in a controlling way that did not allow her to connect with her true self and free herself from her ED. In our sessions, I paid particular attention to how I positioned myself in relation to her in the action part of the process, as I felt the need to have some distance that would allow me to empathise with her without over-identifying and losing my own ability to reflect on what I was experiencing in relation to her in that process. Therefore, I made a conscious decision not to double her body or take on any roles in her dramatisations where I would run the risk of becoming lost myself in my counter-transference. Instead, I tried to help Susanne decode her bodily sensations and body language by pointing out to her what I was noticing in her body language and asking her to exaggerate a movement and then put it into words.

A significant session that helped Susanne decode the language of her body and empathise with it was when I asked her to sculpt with clay how she was experiencing her body. I asked her to place her sculpt at a proximity that represented how far or close she feels in relation to her body. She placed it far away, and the following exploration took place:

THERAPIST: Tell your body how you feel about it.

SUSANNE (TO HER BODY): I don't know what to do with you. I know that you are vulnerable and sick, but I cannot handle you. I don't know if you are my fiend or my enemy. I cannot control you.

I ask Susanne to reverse roles with her body.

BODY: I'm your friend, but you don't always listen to me. So often I'm screaming at you to listen to me and take care of me, but you completely ignore me. When we are in tune, we thrive.

SUSANNE (IN HER ROLE): No, I'm not nice to you, but I don't know how to be nice to you. I've always hated you, because you gave me so much trouble and pain. I don't know how to take care of you, because I feel that you have always been out of control.

BODY: We need some rest together, and we deserve to eat. Listen to me and trust me when I say to you that I'm hungry. When you give me the insulin that I need, I'm happy and you don't have to control me, because you take care of my needs.

SUSANNE: (tearful) I'm proud of you. You've been through so much and you are so courageous and strong. I think you are right. When I listen to you, you protect me. My feelings are my friends. I have to be more compassionate towards my teenage self that went through so much and felt so ashamed and unsafe within you.

BODY: I trust that you can take care of me. You have done it at times recently, and I know that you can continue taking care of my needs. I carry so much shame that is not all mine. Some of it belongs to your bullies and that horrible guy who abused us.

SUSANNE: I promise that I will love you and always try to be in tune with you. I know it's hard at times, but I want you to know that I love you and I'm not going to ignore you anymore.

Working with trauma

As the work progressed and by tracking Susanne's belief system ("I am unworthy," "I am a failure," "Nobody likes me," "I am a disappointment"), we identified its locus nascendi and we began to address her trauma. A significant component of the work we did was focused on Susanne's anger. First of all, I had conceptualised Susanne's secretive ED behaviours as a rebellious and aggressive reaction towards "others" in situations where she could not be the person that the others wanted her to be. This led to a significant exploration of her anger towards her mother, who had very high expectations of her and whose controlling attitude impeded Susanne's development of her own identity and capacity to trust herself. Susanne was very much in tune with the reasons why her mum was not able to mother her more adequately. She often referred to her mother's upbringing as an explanation for the way that she mothered Susanne. Susanne's enmeshment with her mother led to feelings of guilt whenever she became in touch with her anger towards her.

With the use of an empty chair that represented her mother, I asked Susanne to express the feelings and thoughts that her guilt was stopping her from expressing. Susanne began to tentatively express some of her anger, but the role of angry daughter was very new, and she found it hard to fully connect with it. Susanne agreed with my observation that she was trying to be polite and not upset her mother. I used another empty chair behind Susanne's chair, and I asked her to double herself and voice the unedited version of what she had been saying so politely. Susanne finally connected with her anger, and she stood up. She verbalised her anger for various different situations:

> I'm angry with you because you never allowed me to follow my dream and study arts. Studying law was your dream not mine.
>
> I'm angry with you for not being there for me when I was raped.
>
> I'm so angry with you that you never noticed how bad my ED was. That was my way of expressing all this pain for the bullying that I experienced at school.
>
> I'm angry with you because you always took for granted that I was OK.
>
> I'm angry with you for using me as your carer when you were arguing with dad. I became your mother, when I needed to be mothered myself.

After releasing her anger, Susanne created a boundary between her and her mother by using some cloths to symbolise the boundary that she was setting.

Another important encounter was the one that she had with her rapist. We placed an empty chair in the space to locate the rapist role. Susanne chose an object that represented him and put it on the empty chair. She connected with her anger and rage, but she could not verbalise them. I encouraged her to stay connected with her bodily sensations and to express them non-verbally first, as she was finding it very hard to connect with her words. I encouraged her to stand up and gave her cushions that she threw at the chair that represented her rapist, which helped her release some of her anger and rage. Standing up and representing the rapist with only a small object helped her release her anger without feeling threatened or stuck in the role of the victim. This led to her using her voice and her words to express the feelings that up to that time were stuck within her body. She chose a red cloth that represented shame, and she gave it back to him.

In a similar way, she had other encounters with her peers who bullied her at school. Her experience of having to inject insulin at school resulted in her feeling "different" at school, with no sense of belonging. This, paired with being bullied by some of her peers, made her school years traumatic. By accessing her self-compassion for her child and teenage selves and standing up for them, she was empowering her adult self that did not have the need to rebel through ED behaviours in order to survive and cope with painful feelings.

Susanne began to make tangible changes outside the sessions, and her relationships were changing very significantly. She started new hobbies, like creative writing and photography, where she connected with like-minded people. She decided to quit her master's in law and pursue a master's degree in photography.

Towards the later stages of her therapy, Susanne had begun to establish a life of her own. The quality of our therapeutic relationship was changing as Susanne became more confident and able to reclaim her own authority. While in the beginning I felt like I wanted to protect and guide her, I gradually began to withdraw that protection, as she was becoming better able to protect and challenge herself. We began to see each other fortnightly for a few months, and then we reduced the sessions to once a month until she was able to acknowledge that she was ready to end therapy. It is very important for clients who have been traumatised to undergo a process of gradual withdrawal of dependency on the therapist, where they have the opportunity to gradually go through the transition from leaving their safe nest to moving forwards independently.

I feel very privileged to have been a co-traveller on Susanne's journey, which has reiterated my firm belief in people's capacity to grow and recover. It takes a lot of courage to go through the challenging process of recovery, where a sufferer embarks on a journey that takes them to dark places. There is a quote of Friedrich Nietzsche that I think best describes the recovery journey: "One must still have chaos in oneself to be able to give birth to a dancing star" (Nietzsche, 2009).

References

Bloom C, Gitter A, Gutwill S, Kogel L, Zaphiropoulos L. *Eating Problems: A Feminist Psychoanalytic Treatment Model.* New York: Basic Books, 1994.

Brewerton TD. Eating disorders, trauma, and comorbidity: focus on PTSD. *Eating Disorders* 15:285–304, 2007. [PubMed]

Briere J, Scott C Assessment of trauma symptoms in eating-disordered populations. *Eating Disorders* 15:347–358, 2007. [PubMed]

Hillar JR, Lobo MC, Keeling RP. Bulimia and diabetes: a potentially life-threatening combination. *Psychosomatics* 24(3):292–295, 1983.

Hudgins K, Toscani F. *Healing World Trauma with the Therapeutic Spiral Model.* London: Jessica Kingsley, 2013.

Hudson MS, Wentworth SM, Hudson JI. Bulimia and diabetes. *New England Journal of Medicine* 309(7):431–432, 1983.

Jefferies, J. The processing. In M Karp, P Holmes, K Bradshaw Tauvon (eds) *Handbook of Psychodrama.* London: Routledge, 1998.

Moreno JL. *Who Shall Survive?* Second edition. Beacon, NY: Beacon House, 1953.

Moreno JL. The role concept: a bridge between psychiatry and sociology. *American Journal of Psychiatry* 118:518–523, 1961.

Nietzsche F. *Thus Spoke Zarathustra.* Radford, VA: Wilder Publications, 2009.

O'Shaughnessy R, Dallos R. Attachment research and eating disorders: a review of the literature. *Clinical Child Psychology and Psychiatry* 14:559–574, 2009. 10.1177/1359104509339082 [PubMed]

Shapiro R *EMDR Solutions II.* First edition. New York: W.W. Norton, 2009.

Tasca GA, Balfour L. Eating disorders and attachment: a contemporary psychodynamic perspective. *Psychodynamic Psychiatry* 42:257–276, 2014. 10.1521/pdps.2014.42.2.257 [PubMed]

Tribole E, Resch E, *Intuitive Eating: Revolutionary Programme That Works.* New York: St Martin's Griffin, 1995.

Van der Kolk B. *The Body Keeps the Score: Mind, Brain and Body in the Transformation of Trauma.* Harmondsworth, UK: Viking Penguin, 2014.

Zachrisson HD, Skårderud F. Feelings of insecurity: review of attachment and eating disorders. *European Eating Disorders Review* 18:97–106, 2010. 10.1002/erv.999 [PubMed]

Chapter 12

Lucy and her secret inner world

Esther Tang

This chapter is a record of my experience of a psychodramatic journey with a client in Hong Kong called Lucy. She made a big impact on me as she has a sophisticated inner world of multiple roles which she has been directing in a kind of inner drama since childhood. The chapter focuses on my use of the psychodramatic method with this client, whose inner world was evocative of that of someone with dissociative identity disorder (DID).

I am a social worker in Hong Kong, based in a community centre that works with youth with mental health issues. I provide individual and group counselling to the service users. As a social worker, I deal with clients in the role of a case manager who keeps watch over their mental state and social and developmental needs. I develop a care plan that meets such needs by collaborating with other parties involved in the client's life. I arrange relevant groups and activities, including psycho-education for parents and clients, and social exposure activities to avoid clients becoming isolated and consequently suffering a deterioration in their mental state. With certain clients who are motivated towards a deeper understanding of their mental health issues, we provide counselling orientated towards a specific treatment goal.

I first met Lucy when she was 24 years old. She had been diagnosed with depression and was introduced to our service by a friend of hers, who was also a client. She is an attractive, petite young woman, born in Hong Kong. Her father's family immigrated from Macau. She is the only child of a modest-income working-class family.

I have treated her in different phases, firstly in a short-term psychodrama group, then in one-to-one psychodrama psychotherapy, then in a long-term psychodrama psychotherapy group. This chapter focuses mostly on the one-to-one psychotherapy, as part of a process which was later developed in long-term group psychodrama psychotherapy.

Profile of Lucy

Relationship with work, time and money

Lucy brought a number of worries to the counselling room when I first met her. These included her fear of not being able to clear her files quickly enough at work and an inability to tolerate having tasks outstanding at the end of the day, which gave her a strong feeling of failure. She also had a great fear of her boss trying to move her to more challenging jobs in response to her doing well at work. Lucy also put herself under immense pressure to leave the office exactly on time. She was hypervigilant to ensure she would never lose anything, never be taken advantage of, and never spend any money that could be avoided, for example by walking rather taking public transport. She never bought friends drinks or presents, but would very much welcome receiving others' generosity, despite this leading to her being seen as stingy. Lucy had a way of capturing my interest even through the trivial details she told me about her life.

Family background

Lucy's mother had always hoarded recyclable things in their small home, such as newspapers, magazines, metal boxes and cans. She collected these and tried to sell them to earn more money, although both parents had paid jobs. Father always complained about the home being occupied by mother's stuff, as mother sold it at a much slower rate than collecting it. The couple often got into heated arguments as father was hot-tempered and easily irritated by things he found unreasonable, while mother was rigid about her peculiar judgements and decisions. Little Lucy felt devastated by their endless conflicts. Even now she would cry secretly every time they quarrelled. Father was also very intolerant of any minor mischief or mistake of little Lucy. He would be instantly infuriated and left Lucy in a state of extremely high anxiety. However, one could never tell what was going on inside Lucy as she had learnt to suppress her responses. If she cried or whined, father would become more terrifying. Mother had a more controlled temper, so Lucy was able talk to her, but only in an unnatural way. As a child, Lucy talked to her by holding a plush toy bird pretending it was "Birdie" talking to mother, and Lucy was still doing this as an adult. From mother's point of view, this was intimate mother–child talk. To Lucy, it was her way of keeping a distance from her mother, who she saw as uncompromising. Mother would cook at a late hour because she had to follow her after-work routine of reading, organising her stuff and resting before cooking the family meal. She was very devoted to Lucy's learning tasks. She had little Lucy read and view a lot of English learning books and videos, and insisted Lucy needed to make use of every moment to learn, including toilet time. She had a habit of continuing doing dictation practice with Lucy even when either one of them needed to go to the toilet, by half-opening the toilet door. Lucy did not recognise this as pressure until much later. Although mother was not particularly happy or angry when Lucy did well or badly at a test, Lucy remembered mother's disappointment with her when she got 98% and coached her to ensure she would get the 100% she deserved. Another reason why Lucy felt unable to trust mother was that mother always backed father up when he scolded her even in an unreasonably fierce manner for a child. At one time, father threw a box at the wall beside Lucy due to a minor mischief, mother heard father's scolding, but just stayed in the kitchen as if nothing had happened, then told them to clear the table. Many a time like this, Lucy would just go to the toilet and cry.

Ambivalent yearning for closeness

Lucy appeared polite, friendly, scrupulous and obedient in most of her real-life social circles. She had been a member of a particular online forum where she had a completely different character. There she was wild and open in expressions full of foul and sexually obsessed language. She was socially active online and had many virtual friends.

Lucy easily developed crushes on men, especially those who presented in a child-like way. She had tried to develop a relationship with a more mature and steady colleague, but he was unable to accept her child-like moments of fear and viewed her as immature. The relationship broke up.

Lucy's secret: dissociative identity disorder?

Lucy had no intention of revealing a secret she had held for almost 20 years when she came into therapy, as she thought it was too weird to be comprehended by anybody. She revealed it to me after around 20 sessions of individual therapy.

She told me this story. Since around age seven, without remembering exactly what had happened before, she noticed that a few internal "people" were emerging. One of them, here called Captain, was the creator of a system. He told her that they were orphans from abroad, and Lucy had fallen into such a deep sleep that she could not be found any more. They were to share the job of being Lucy.

Captain made up a grid-like roster: there would always be two people in the front line and two backstage in support. One of the two in the front line would take up the role of Lucy that people could see, the other one in the front line was a partner that others could not see. The partner would talk to her internally, or out loud if Lucy was alone. One way they interacted was that the partner would be on the right side of Lucy's body. Lucy could shift between the two parts or lean in to the "partner" for comfort.

The people backstage usually had special talents or functions and only came out when needed. For example, one of them took the nurse's role to take care of Lucy when she was wounded, and one was a "smarty" who could solve maths problems.

The cast of the internal workers changed over time. If Captain thought the frontline role was not fit for the job, someone else would be shifted to the front. As time went on, more and more workers were created, some of the old ones would appear again, but some of them would be lost forever. There would also be discussion among the workers about who would be at the front. The system held a rule that no one should disclose it to any human beings, and no one could fall in love with a real human. They could only fall in love with each other.

When Lucy was a teenager, a frontline worker called Lily had a crush on a boy in class. Having broken the rule of no real relationships, she was fired. Then a worker called Hana was told to be Lucy. Ever since then, Hana held that role. The internal crew even told Hana that she could just become Lucy, since no one knew how to find her ever again.

As Lucy grew up, the number of internal workers gradually came down to only three, namely Hana, Lily and Ed. Ed was Lucy's soulmate/boyfriend. There were quite a few adventures and love stories among the workers. They could even have imagined sex with each other. When Lucy was around 18, the rule of not falling in love with real humans was no longer held. Hana had crushes on teachers and other boys. The workers would try to support Hana to do what was needed to move on with the relationship.

Although the system was less rigorous than before, Lucy did not know how to operate in the world without it. Hana had taken up the mask of Lucy, and the real Lucy was already lost in space. Unsurprisingly, this made her feel abnormal. She got into trouble when dealing with intimate relationships, as being human felt like a job to her. The relationship could never quite be as safe as with her internal boyfriends. At times of conflict, she would quickly withdraw to her own world and cry.

This story was never told to psychiatrists. There was no formal diagnosis whether Lucy's experience of inner roles was on the spectrum of DID. DID is characterised by having "highly discrete states of consciousness organised around a prevailing affect, sense of self (including body image), with a limited repertoire of behaviours and a set of state dependent memories" (Putnam, 1989:103). Lucy referred to herself as "they" when she disclosed her truth, and her inner roles felt like separate real persons and seemed to have enduring individual characters, ages and ways of being. The different roles rarely changed their characteristics and integrated with each other. She only experienced new roles coming in and old ones going somehow according to need and changes in life. They just emerged and faded away, apparently of their own accord. Also, it felt to Lucy that the inner roles just took over her body, which had become a shell that faces the world, hosting the different parts of self who filled in to be in the executive control as needed. This is known as switching to the "alter" identity states (Howell, 2011).

There are many variations of DID, and there can be partial dissociation, which seems to be Lucy's category. Lucy did not have dissociative amnesia in shifting between alters. In her case, the alters worked as a team; they coexisted simultaneously to take up duties seamlessly and could give Lucy different perspectives like in a group discussion.

The function of Lucy's system was to protect herself from her parents' intense emotional reactivity towards each other and herself. She needed this dissociative coping mechanism to keep a psychological distance from her parents and the mess of feelings that were not understood by her parents.

How the therapeutic relationship began

Lucy presented for relational group counselling. In the group, she shared about anxiety in relating with colleagues, how she would rather isolate herself than see them mingling closer than she was, how she was anxious about her boss's expectations and how she could not bear a junior who was not following her instructions. After the group experience, she requested individual counselling. She frequently telephoned me about stressful situations at work. Her anxiety settled for a while, then the dependent pattern of calling for soothing would reoccur. It seemed clear that I had become her attachment figure. I then invited her to be a short-term psychodrama group client, then my individual psychodrama client. I reframed our relationship as therapist and client instead of a problem solving social worker and restructured our sessions to be regular weekly face-to-face therapy. Lucy followed this structure very well, and she learnt to contain her emotions for a week at a time instead of calling helplessly and feeling overwhelmed incessantly.

Assessment and initial phase

During assessment, small objects in the form of spectogram, timeline and social atoms were used to familiarise Lucy with the psychodramatic method. Her relationship with other people was concretised spatially, chronologically and with multi-perspectives. Her way of interpreting others' viewpoint was also assessed through role reversal with different people. In the process, I recognised and reflected to her that her intense anxiety about fulfilling the demands of others was out of proportion with the stimulus in reality, and probably was rooted in early childhood experience. She felt understood by me, while all her colleagues and existing friends could not really understand why she would get so anxious. The feeling of being different from others extended to almost all relationships with others. Lucy did not have a lot of friends, she felt she was just performing in socially acceptable ways without genuinely relating with people, although she behaved in a chatty and clingy way with certain friends. Her only emotionally strong moments were when her friends put themselves in situations of being taken advantage of by other people, which was puzzling to herself as well. In my countertransference, I had great personal resonance with her distanced style of interpersonal relating, a resonance which I believe enhanced the therapeutic alliance.

Turning point

Throughout the one-to-one sessions, it became clear that she wore a mask in all her interpersonal relationships, a smiling agreeable mask that made her seem harmless. Yet behind this mask was a ferocious anger and deep sadness that could not be shown to most people.

Every time we explored the mask to hear its message, Lucy showed great pain. It was always painful for her to recognise her mask but feel there was no way to remove it. I deduced with Lucy that the mask was developed at a young age to avoid provoking her hot-tempered father and as a response to mother's lack of mirroring .

The psychodramatic encounter with Lucy's mask laid the groundwork for a deeper level of intervention. The disclosure of her secret internal system came at a moment when I reflected back to her the deep pain I sensed at her needing to hold on to a mask which left her ultimately disconnected from others.

The mask represented the internal system for Lucy. The intervention work was based on the following role analysis. In situations when she was under distress to fulfil role expectations from the outer world, she used her mask to behave acquiescently and the internal team system to frenetically solve the problems. Inside, she was feeling devastated, extremely worried, and a sense of dread (or hatred if it was towards her parents). She believed her authentic being was too vulnerable and unable to bear the hardship and demands from the world, and her true feelings would be unappreciated by others and were obstructing her performance in the eyes of others, and could only be "shared" internally within the system. The consequence was an estrangement from her true self, and from people in the world.

Psychodramatic method

Her contact with the psychodramatic method was painfully revealing for her. Role reversal and concretising different internal roles inside reminded her of her internal structure, but also her aloneness. She desperately wished for someone who had the same experience as her. In role reversal with others, she could do the task, but with a sense that it was not real, just like any fake encounter with others in her daily life. In getting into the role of another, she had difficulty feeling what they felt. I came to understand that she had a kind of shield that stopped her connecting to others, with the belief that unless someone could understand her as well as her internal system, she should protect herself from them and keep them as a distanced object.

I sometimes wondered if the embodied method of psychodrama was too painful a reminder of her difference from others. For her, the existence of multiple inner roles was a more literal reality and necessity for survival, not, as for most people, the luxury of experimenting with a creative psychotherapeutic method.

Yet this method served her deep desire to share her world with others as vividly as possible. Her world of internal helpers really was created by a young child's soul in search of support and resonance.

Also, the method was a good rehearsal for her to practise authentic communication with others, in terms of role training to communicate with real people.

Achievements in one-to-one sessions carrying on to long-term group therapy

Lucy experienced gradual improvements, firstly through tasting psychodrama in a short-term group, then moving on to 40 sessions of one-to-one therapy, and finally into a long-term group, as discussed below.

Psychodrama served as a bridge for Lucy to move on from relying on support from her internal world to experimenting with the external world. In the process of struggling between trusting her inner team only and letting real people into her world, Lucy had broken through her taboo about revealing her internal system with the therapist, then other real people. Towards the end of one-to-one therapy, Lucy asked her cousin to come to a therapy session to share the secret. She felt supported by her cousin and less alone in the world. After that, she also told this story to some strangers on a helpline. This experience somewhat reduced her distance with real people.

After 15 sessions of the long-term group, she told the members about this secret, and after that she also told an old school teacher. It was a sign of self-acceptance to be able to share with more people.

In individual sessions, she explored her distaste when her parents asked her to pay them a bigger allowance as there was greater financial stress in the family. In Chinese culture, it sounds reasonable for an adult child to share the burden of the family when it is in financial difficulty. However, Lucy had always wanted to flee from her family instead of being needed by it. She was repulsed by the idea that her parents were expecting her to be a loving, dutiful daughter, although on the surface she seemed compliant in this respect. We used the psychodramatic method of the empty chair encounter to express her hidden hatred towards her parents. This intervention helped release some tension inside her, as in real life she never told her parents any of her feelings.

Issues tackled

Parental transference towards authority figures

Lucy functioned very well at work, but she often got stressed by her bosses' responses to her, while also being very attached to the working environment. In one-to-one sessions, we explored encountering various line managers on the empty chair. We could recognise and concretise her paternal transference towards the more demanding ones. In another case, she had an idealising mother transference towards a female boss, which resulted in great distress when that manager became slightly cross with her on occasion. In both cases, she was very threatened by emotional changes in authority figures. That caused her to be reluctant to take promotions as she feared she might no longer perform perfectly in the eyes of her bosses and colleagues. We also discovered that she had a similar transference towards her boyfriend. When the relationship started, they both acted and talked to each other in a childish, intimate manner which she enjoyed. As the relationship went on and they started to talk about more serious things, she found her boyfriend not very tolerant of some of her spontaneous childish remarks and behaviour. Lucy started to feel pressured to avoid disapproval from him just as with her parents. Being more aware of the transference of situation, Lucy gradually became less affected by situations when such people got angry.

Lucy's trust towards me in bringing her secret issues was probably also based on an idealising parental transference. I represented someone who could be calm and attune to her inner world, much like how her internal system served her. Later, when she was in the long-term group, I received angry attacks from her in which she reported that she was only going through the motions at moments of some psychodramatic intervention when she considered that intervention to be beyond her capacity. At these times, I was seen as an unattuned, demanding mother. This could be seen as a sign of improvement in her expressing disagreement with me as an authority while still managing to maintain the relationship.

The difficulty in role reversal with family

Lucy was reluctant to reverse roles with her parents. She was immensely sad at having to pretend to be a good, submissive daughter while hiding so much hatred inside her, even fantasising about killing her parents or escaping home from a young age. Metaphors of imprisoned life always made her cry. Thinking of this, it made sense why the creator of her internal system, Captain, told her that the internal workers were orphans kidnapped from abroad. Her life was a show for her parents. She was internally estranged from them since childhood and felt that she could not let the parents, who felt like "kidnappers", know that she wanted to escape or she would risk a terrible consequence.

Lucy grew up feeling she was all alone whenever she faced difficulties. She believed she could not be herself in front of her family. She was only acting like the girl her parents wanted to have. Thus, to her, being Lucy was a job. The only time she was authentic was when she was alone, the only people she could feel real with were her internal workers. Lucy carried this model of internal and external world everywhere she went. Even when with her friends and teachers at school, she still thought it was Lucy's job to just act like normal people. In addition, little Lucy knew her family was not normal because of her mother's hoarding problem and her parents' continuous rows. Lucy's internal world then became her surrogate family, friends and lovers that were more fulfilling and reliable than any real ones. With this system going on for years, the feeling of having something so different from everybody else kept her in self-segregation with the belief she was an abnormal species. This was especially problematic when it came to intimate relationships, which Lucy longed for. When she was young, she fantasised about romance because of her loneliness. When she approached adulthood, it meant more. She wished a man could come and marry her to rescue her from the family, which would be the only imaginable way for her to escape her issues with the family, as it was unimaginable for her to truly talk to them openly from her heart.

As our one-to-one sessions progressed towards her core issues of expressing authentic feelings to others, this inevitably linked back to the problems within the family. Lucy was eager to tell her stories from the past, but she found it dreadful to take on the roles of her parents, especially her father. She could only do this by doubling the empty chair representing father. This distancing technique allowed her to be a voice over, rather than "being" him. Her difficulty in playing the angry father may also reflect the rigid and limited role repertoire in her predominant alters, which is common in DID. Lucy's existing alters were formed to present a submissive personality to help her survive in the face of father's uncontrolled temper. Lucy had mentioned there once was an alter who could display more aggressive behaviour, but was already lost. It was valuable that Lucy could have some psychodramatic role training to widen her role repertoire.

The challenge of romantic relationship

The first emotionally intense relationship we worked on in one-to-one sessions was with her first boyfriend. We explored her feeling of having hurt him, reducing him to tears in front of her after one week of dating when she told him that she realised she did not like him. The incident was six years ago, but she still felt immense guilt as we processed the emotions through encounter. The guilt was painfully felt as if the pain was inflicted on herself. This had been the first instance of her awareness of hurting another person, and it deterred her from another relationship for several years.

Lucy could handle loneliness most of the time as she had her internal pals to comfort her and discuss things with when facing problems. Her loneliness and hopelessness would be intensified when she found herself attracted to someone romantically. She had a difficult experience in going through her second relationship with a man who attracted her as a responsible person, but who failed to show understanding of her at her low times. She used the one-to-one sessions to prepare to tell him her secret, although eventually she chose to break up without telling it. During those sessions, she engaged with her need to work on letting go of her internal friends and invest in real-life relationships.

When she embarked on her third potential relationship, she was trapped in a dilemma. If she held on to her internal boyfriend who would never hurt her, she would be safe, but would feel abnormal the rest of her life. If she ventured to develop a real relationship, she was risking hurt, disappointment, rejection. She made use of a newly learnt voice gained from her one-to-one sessions which encouraged her to try not holding on too much to her internal friends, but to seek authentic connection with real people. When she began the third potential relationship, she told him the secret, in the hope of starting it authentically. It was not received positively, which was painful for her, but it was evidence that she was beginning to adopt new responses to facing the world.

Lucy's process in the long-term group

The long-term group Lucy joined consisted of five women in their early twenties. The cohesion and mutual trust and support were built up quite successfully in the first few sessions. Lucy's worry that the group could not replace me as her individual therapist largely faded away as she realised it was a group that she could trust and share with. Her familiarity with the psychodramatic method and psychological/emotional literacy gained through one-to-one sessions helped her lower her anxiety. In session 16, Lucy disclosed her secret of having an internal system to the group by doing a piece of work in which she concretised her roster system and the key internal "friends" onstage. The one-to-one sessions had worked like a rehearsal for her to come into contact with other human beings more authentically. She was anxious and excited to hear the sharing of the group afterwards. Their calm and understanding response and partial resonance were a relief, although also a disappointment to her. On the one hand she did not want people to judge her as abnormal, on the other hand she wanted people to recognise the damage she bore, which kept her desolate and separated from the world.

In subsequent sessions, Lucy felt closer to the group, and could bring in the hidden side of her and her internal world onto the psychodrama stage. Although the group still had not replaced the internal system in terms of intimate support, it was a test for both Lucy and the group of how much authenticity they could bring to each other.

Lucy felt weird about herself not having the same human to human affection as others. In the group, she gradually confessed more and more of her difference with others, including what she called the "evil" part of her. She shared her experience of behaving like a real, concerned, listening friend to her friends while knowing she was not doing it from her heart, but as a performance of expected social norms, sometimes with the manipulative intention of being treated generously by friends. Later on, she disclosed to the group about her ideation of harming others. She believed this aspect was pathological and was seeking to be released from it. We learned that her compliant "be good" outward behaviour was learnt through harsh discipline from father and the quarrels between her parents. This not only built up suppressed hatred towards her parents, but also seemed to have blocked the development of natural moral compassion. Recognition of the link between her perceived immoral and harmful intent towards real people and the unexpressed hatred towards her parents helped her understand and accept herself better and created a resonance within the group.

In one of Lucy's psychodramas, I got the chance to interview her internal boyfriend. I got the feeling that "he" did not have his own view about things, he only served a function for Lucy as her object that gave and received intimate love. I got a deeper understanding that it was only safe for her to relate to objects, just as she had adopted a habit to talk to stuffed toys since she was a toddler. Real humans could get explosively angry like her father, and unattuned and indifferent like her mother, and rejecting and not understanding like her previous boyfriends and friends. It seemed it was also her experience to have been treated like a thing by her parents, who took care of her physically and academically without listening to and feeling what was inside her. This estranged relationship with people was all she had, and the relationship with the always good love objects inside her could never be transferable to real relationships. There seemed no natural pathway for her to be truly connected affectionately and affectively with human beings. To learn to do so felt to her like an alien trying to learn to be human. The pain and hopeless feeling that came from this attempt would prompt her to go back to the internal world as the best protection. This ongoing shifting between going outward from and inward towards her internal world had been witnessed through her journey. It would take huge courage and support from therapy to take steps out of the struggle.

Change in her internal system

At the beginning of therapy, Lucy had three internal friends, as mentioned above. One was Hana, who took up the heaviest job of facing the world, one was Lily, who was like a co-worker with her since teenage years, one was a male soulmate, Ed, who was both like a boyfriend and a calm, wise person. In the middle of her individual therapy, Lily was reported to have faded away gradually, and Hana missed her. After a number of psycho-drama group sessions, Lucy told the group that her soulmate Ed had also disappeared, which surprised me as he had been a very important support to her for many years. Lucy said she had to make an effort to call out an old internal boyfriend to accompany her after she was hurt in the third potential relationship. I inferred from this change that the therapist, the group and more positive relationships in real life had served some functions of the internal friends and wise person. However, she would revert to the use of an internal boyfriend if she was disillusioned by a romantic relationship. Perhaps the only way to replace this internal role would be to find a sustainable intimate relationship in the real world.

Lucy's quest to reclaim the disowned self

Lucy had been interacting with me and the world with the identity of Hana, and occasionally other internal workmates, but never as the original Lucy. Her system had disowned the original sense of self in order to insulate herself from the mess of feelings towards her parents. Her pain was tackled by "others" through the system she had created in her psyche. Operating through surrogate selves to share the pressure of facing her parents had also preserved a functional, maintainable relationship with them for the sake of survival. In psychodramatic interventions, Lucy had the understanding that she would have to learn to reduce the use of her internal system. However, if functioning as Hana or any other identity, she could not possibly let go of the system as she was part of it. In a piece of psychodrama where she attempted to be in role as Lucy, prior to the system coming into being, the role had become so unfamiliar that she had to use her imagination to try to be the original Lucy. In that piece of work, the imagined original Lucy had the wish to delete the system and to reclaim her own identity, although she did not know how to do so as she had lost the ability to really be the original self again instead of being the created personalities. It would require future effort to help Lucy get in touch with the original self.

Conclusion

With Lucy's case, I have learnt that a clever child's over-investment in a dissociative coping method can snowball into a monstrously debilitating mechanism. The mechanism could perfectly protect the child from hurt, which made it hard for her to give it up and risk the unpredictability in the world of real human relationship. The more she was encapsulated within her system, the less willing she became to be empathetic with the human world, a world which came to be seen as a thing or object for her to get what she needs from and discharge her hatred towards. On the other hand, when she started to develop more trusting relationships with others, she showed herself capable of a more prosocial connection to others. It will take great perseverance from her to sustain such effort instead of falling back into withdrawal and discounting all the authentic moments in relationship that she has developed.

Lucy expressed gratitude to have had the opportunity to experience psychodrama psychotherapy both individually and as a group method. It had given her a more thorough understanding of herself, and an option to not just jump into seeing herself as an abnormal and pitiful creature. She could see a possibility that she could gradually learn to express her true feelings to others and revise her internal system. She hoped that she might eventually learn to live as a fellow human being belonging to the world.

References

Howell, E. (2011). *Understanding and Treating Dissociative Identity Disorder: A Relational Approach*. New York: Routledge.

Putnam, F. W. (1989). *The Diagnosis and Treatment of Multiple Personality Disorder*. New York: Guilford Press.

Chapter 13

A brief one-to-one session using role analysis and role theory in a corporate organisation

Maxine Daniels

Introduction

This chapter explores working with a manager in a one-to-one session as part of a drop-in clinic in a large insurance company. The drop-in clinic was organised by the company in order to support the staff, who were working at full capacity because there had been flooding in the North of England, where many families had been displaced and buildings, along with businesses, had been destroyed. It was a crisis situation, and as a result the manager in the session was de-motivated and struggling to support her staff team. In this chapter, I highlight the use of psychodrama techniques, role analysis, role theory and how to work in a brief one-to-one session. To try to help you, the reader, make sense of the chapter, I have structured it under repetitive headings: "My thinking", in which I write about diagnosis, role analysis and decision making, and "The session", where I write about the interventions, content and the use of psychodrama techniques.

Background information

Whilst I am a qualified psychodrama psychotherapist, my work is very varied and I work across the spectrum from corporate organisations to public sector companies delivering training using action techniques. I also engage in clinical work supervising staff in prisons and hospitals with themes ranging from offending behaviour treatment programmes to mental health. I tend to use psychodrama psychotherapy in different ways dependent on the environment I am working in. On this particular occasion, I used my psychotherapy psychodrama skills in a brief one-to-one meeting, which bordered on a therapeutic coaching session, but with an understanding that I would most probably only meet the client once.

My arrival at the company for the one-to-one session

On the particular day I arrive at the insurance company, an imposing new building with the name of the company blazoned across the front, I have no idea what I will be met with. At reception, I am signed in, given my security badge and directed to the lift, where I am told to take it to the third floor and head for room 3.05. I step out of the lift into a large open-plan office where there is a lot of noise as people are speaking on the phones. I stop and ask someone if they can point me in the right direction to room 3.05. I get to the room, which is quite small with big windows and lots of light, and whilst it is at the end of the big open-plan office, it has frosted glass between the room and the office, meaning no one can see in. There is a table with a chair either side of it and a spare chair in the corner. In my bag I have brought a few props, a couple of soft toys, a few small multi-coloured scarves, lots of A4 paper and pens with a few sheets of flipchart paper. These are the tools of the trade, and I never arrive without A4 paper and marker pens to any session because they always come in handy. The door opens and a friendly woman asks if I would like a coffee and hands me a piece of paper with names of the staff who will be coming to see me. During this day I am going to meet about five people all booked in for an hour each with space and time in between. I may have met some of them before, but I have no idea if they have been on a training programme with a colleague of mine who delivers a suite of programmes to staff about mental health, well being and resilience or if they have attended the days when I have delivered the programmes. It has been agreed with management that if anyone would like extra support, they can use this "drop-in clinic" to seek help. As I wait in the room, I have no idea who will walk through the door or the issue they will bring with them, only that it will be linked to work and the issues they are currently struggling with in the company.

Background to the work: environmental issues

Prior to my "drop-in clinic", there had been a deluge of storms and floods in this part of the UK. Members of the public were in a distressed state, calling the insurance company to seek financial payments to help them. Families had lost their homes and were living in temporary accommodation, emergency services were stretched and struggling to cope, people had died, and many were in hospital. This is the backdrop to the working environment of the staff currently dealing with the claimants. These claimants were often traumatised and desperately seeking help to find alternative accommodation and resources.

The one-to-one session

After waiting for 5 minutes in the room, the door opens and a woman in her early 30s greets me in a low voice, "Hello I'm Fiona, I'm the manager, I'm here for the drop-in clinic, is this the right place?" I notice immediately that Fiona looks "heavy", as if she is carrying the weight of the world on her shoulders, and there is a sense of vulnerability about her.

"Hello, I'm Maxine, I'm leading the drop-in clinic today, good to meet you," I smile at her. I am aware that I am already feeling some kind of connection with her, and I sense her vulnerability working in this challenging environment. She continues, "I'm not sure you can help, but I thought I've got nothing to lose, which is why I've booked onto this session." I respond to her, "Well, something helped you to find your way here, so maybe you can tell me what it is, and if I can help in any way, I'll try." She takes a seat at the table and suddenly bursts into tears:

> I've never experienced anything like it, people are phoning all the time, the phones never stop ringing, it's just awful, they've lost their homes, they have nowhere to live, customers are really distressed, flooding, buildings flooded, they even have to go through re-validation of their professional work to get medical care … it's awful.

I offer her a tissue and wait. In those few minutes, I recognise that Fiona is "warmed up" to the issues she has been holding in relation to work and she has already told me the presenting problem: demands from people who are in a distressed state in relation to the flooding. In this short exchange, I have got the essence of the problem. She continues, "I feel so helpless, I can't help them, I should be able to do something." I feel incredibly moved by her presence and her feelings of helplessness. I recognise this is not just about myself and Fiona in that room at that particular time, it is about the universe, the cosmos and facing life-and-death issues. I think about Jacob Moreno, the founding father of psychodrama, and the title of his book, *Who Shall Survive?* (1953). I recognise this is a global phenomenon: severe weather conditions affecting populations all over the world. In this short space of time, I reflect on this and role reverse in my mind with all the individuals trying to get help with insurance claims and the people who are suffering from the environmental crisis. No wonder Fiona feels so overwhelmed.

My thinking: role analysis

In my training at the London Centre for Psychodrama Group and Individual Psychotherapy, Jinnie Jefferies, the founder of the school, developed "role analysis" (Goldman & Morrison 1984; Bustos 1994; Jefferies 2004), and this template has stood me in good stead throughout my time as a therapist, coach and supervisor in a variety of situations. It is immediately accessible, and helps me to diagnose the client and the situation and to think about the interventions I can make. The template consists of the following:

Context – What is the specific situation the protagonist (client) is encountering – in other, words what is the *other* doing or what is happening *to* the client.

Behaviour – In response to this situation, how is the client behaving?
Feeling – What are their feelings in this specific situation?
Beliefs – What are the beliefs they hold about self, other and the world that are driving the behaviour in this specific situation?
Consequences – Finally what are the consequences of this? What is the maladaptive behaviour or response that will emerge? And how do I help them to correct this?

The session

"I can't make it OK, I can't make it better," Fiona interrupts my thought. "Whatever I say, they have still lost their homes and loved ones, it's awful, if only I could do something, I should be able to help." I can see the heaviness weighing her down as her body sinks further into the chair. However, my ears prick up when I hear Fiona say, "I should be able to help," because unbeknown to her, she is giving me a fundamental insight into her feelings of heaviness.

My thinking

Words such as "should" are a clue in helping me to understand her thoughts in relation to the situation because they are related to her "belief system", a learned attitude, or way of seeing the world and traced back to a much younger self.

Young (1999) refers to this belief system as schema, a concept used in cognitive behavioural therapy. Within this moment, I realise the "heaviness" Fiona is carrying is probably linked to "responsibility" which she has possibly learnt in her distant past, a belief that she needs to take care of others in their distress. Hence the message "I should" be able to do something. The self-sacrifice schema SS (Young 1999) is one of a list of 18 schemas that Young cites, and one of the most common reasons for this particular schema is to stop causing pain to others, or to avoid feeling guilty, because this schema operates by giving the client an acute sensitivity to the pain of others. I am wondering if this applies to Fiona in her personal or professional role, does she have an acute sense of responsibility? The crisis of the current situation could certainly tap into this. In this short time, Fiona has exposed her innermost thoughts, which helps me to formulate a diagnosis and find out where the problem may be.

The session

Fiona reaches for another tissue, which I have placed on the table. She is shaking her head and lowers it with the words, "I can't stop thinking about

Working with role analysis in an organisation   173

it, even when I'm at home, I go over and over how I can help them, news stories on TV make it much worse as well." I recognise that Fiona could be verging on secondary trauma (Tehrani 2011), experiencing the distress of others through burnout and a sense of helplessness, or she could be blurring her personal "caring" role with her professional management role. I look at the clock on the wall, and given that Fiona was 5 minutes late, I realise a good 15 minutes have already passed by, so I need to start making decisions about how to manage this session.

My thinking

We have, at most, 30 minutes to work in action, with a good 10 to 15 minutes to "cool down" and for sharing, so I am wondering what is the best way to help Fiona at this moment in time. She may need further support, or she may need to seek counselling if the images prove to be secondary trauma that she is experiencing. However, it could be an inability to "detach" herself from the human stories she is exposed to, and my job will be to help her understand that she is not solely responsible for the current crisis in this part of the UK. In my head, I return to my role analysis to make sense of what I have heard.

Context (specific situation) – in a work situation where demands are being made of her from distressed others in crisis;
Behaviour – she tries to help to put policies into place, tries to detach herself emotionally, becomes tearful, and is preoccupied with the collective trauma;
Feelings she feels overwhelmed, upset, helpless and alone;
Beliefs – she has a duty to help, which is endless; her responsibility is limitless, with no support from anyone else, and only she can stop the distress;
Consequences – she tries to keep to the boundary of work, but feels overwhelmed with the belief that she should resolve the crisis for them and then ruminates on the victims' distress out of work.

I check my own evidence about this role analysis. Is it true that only Fiona can sort it out? I want to observe Fiona's specific response, in action, in her role of manager when being confronted with the distress of others if she believes that only she can help and her sense of responsibility is limitless (Bustos 1994). I am also wondering about role conflict for Fiona. We might need to do some "internal separation" of roles between her "personal" sensitive role and her "professional" management role. The sensitive role has a strong belief that she personally is responsible, whilst the professional role can work within the boundaries of the company, offering advice. I am aware of time, and decide to place out two chairs to check the role analysis first.

The session: action

I place out two chairs in the small room opposite each other, and I write "Customer" and "Manager" on separate pieces of A4 paper, placing them next to each chair. I ask Fiona to come and stand next to me, explaining that I want her to show me what happened in the telephone call with the customer so I can get further understanding of the situation and how she responded, in order to help her. I continue speaking to her, and knowing I want her alongside me to try and overcome any resistance, I say:

> I know this may feel strange, Fiona, to ask you to stand up and then sit back down on one of these chairs and take on the role of customer and manager, but I'm asking if you'll just go with it so we can try to make sense of what's happening to you.

In my experience, clients who have never engaged in psychodrama techniques feel very strange when asked to stand, let alone engage with all sorts of moving exercises we know as action methods in psychodrama. Fiona looks at me and slowly rises from the chair with a look of suspicion and comes to stand next to me. I am aware at this point it is about the "relational" aspect of the work (Rogers 1980; Mearns & Cooper 2018): if she does not feel safe with me, she will not engage in the exercises or the "as if" (Vaihinger 1924; Kellerman 1992) of the scene. I explain the position of the two chairs, and say to her:

> I want you to sit in the chair marked "Manager", that's you, and show me what happens when the phone rings and what the customer says to you, so when you take the seat, I will speak to you *as if* it is happening now. Don't worry about getting names right, or remembering everything in the exchange, it's just to get an idea of what was said in the conversation with the customer.

I give her my mobile to use as a prop, and continue to explain, "Let's go to the point where the customer speaks and it becomes difficult for you." I also clarify with Fiona that I am not here in this capacity to engage with the policies of the company, that is not my job. Often clients in organisations want to talk about company policy, so it is really important to spell this out and tell them we are not focusing on policies, but on the relational and human interactions. Fiona sits in the chair marked "Manager", holding the mobile phone, and I direct her, "OK – let's hear what you say to this person on the other end of the phone in your role of manager." Initially she looks blank, and then begins to speak slowly to me, "I think she told me she has three kids and they've lost their home, the flooding was so bad, I sit and listen and then find it difficult to speak." I ask, "Do you say anything?" She replies, "I can't remember." At this point, in order to keep the "as if", I direct her to speak to the empty chair, "You're speaking to the customer, imagine she is sitting in the chair and is on the phone, let's hear what happens." Fiona goes through the routine of introducing herself to the customer, giving her name and job title, and asks how she may help. I ask her, "Do you say anything else here?" Fiona stops, "No, I don't get the chance because she (pointing to the chair) starts to shout at me."

Role reversing with the customer

I ask her to role reverse with the customer. She obligingly stands up and takes the other chair. Fiona, in the role of customer, looks at the empty chair (manager chair) slightly puzzled, but there is something about sitting in the role of the customer that begins to take effect, the simple act of role reversing with the other has an impact. From the role of customer, Fiona's voice suddenly rises an octave and she cries out, "I've got three kids, the water just kept pouring in, I thought we were going to drown, I've lost my home, I don't know what to do, please help me, you need to do something." Then silence.

I look at the woman sitting in the chair speaking to the insurance company. I see a woman with three children and her desperation at losing her home. The action is very powerful, and I have to check myself that I do not get drawn into the emotion, but keep the role analysis in mind to help Fiona focus on her "professional role" in order to help the customer.

In manager role

I say to Fiona, "Let's bring you out of this chair, can you stand up please?" Fiona follows my instructions, "Are you OK?" I ask, and she nods her head. "I'm now going to ask you to take your role as the manager again and show me how you respond to this statement." She continues to work with me, and I praise her to support her, "Well done, it's beginning to make sense to me," and I direct her to respond to the statement that had previously been made by the customer. I repeat her statement from a distance whilst she is on the phone (prop) to the customer. At the end of the statement, Fiona says, "I'm sorry, I'm so sorry, that's awful." Pause. Fiona has now slumped into the chair and looks at me, "This is terrible, it must be really difficult for her family, nothing will help." I'm now curious about the rest of the role analysis. "How do you feel here?" I ask her. "Terrible, just terrible, I feel responsible somehow for making it better for her, I feel helpless, heavy," she replies. "Is that the feeling of responsibility?" Fiona responds with, "Yes, yes, it is, I feel responsible for her and her family." "And what about the thought you mentioned earlier, that you 'should' be able to help her?" I direct her to look at the chair with "Customer" written on it. We both look at the customer chair, and again there is a long pause. Fiona, in a quiet voice and tearful again, says, "Yes, I should be able to make it better, and all I can do is direct her to the website to try and make a claim."

My thinking

I am wondering at this stage whether part of Fiona's helplessness is to do with the large organisation, and maybe the organisational policies are so hostile that claimants are not able to get the help they need and this exacerbates her feelings of helplessness. So I decide to check this out with her.

The session

"You talk about what you think you 'should' be doing here, Fiona, can I just ask you about the insurance policies in relation to these claimants? Are they able to claim on them, or are they being turned away?" Fiona looks at me, "No, they're not being turned away, the company has been really good in trying to resolve things quickly, it's just a difficult process for people when they're already struggling." This is helpful information to me, because now I recognise that she believes the company is doing its part to help, it is not so much about external factors, but more about Fiona's locus of control, her relationship with herself. This is an intra-psychic piece of work for Fiona – in other words, it is her thinking, beliefs and feelings that drive her behaviour in which she goes round and round in circles, never being able to resolve it for herself. We have spent about 10 minutes in the action, and with time pressing, I am now thinking it is important for Fiona to be able to move forward. So what to do in the time we have left? Check my role analysis again.

My thinking

Role analysis

Context – in a situation where the distressed other is making demands on Fiona to do something to help them.
Behaviour – Fiona tries to help them, but is overwhelmed by the distress and gives up;
Feelings – sad, upset, helpless, responsible and alone;
Beliefs – in her role of manager, she believes she should be able to sort it out and make it better, and only she can make it better;
Consequences – she is left with a heavy feeling of not being able to help them as much as she should, and then ruminates later.

Working with role analysis in an organisation 177

Because this is a present situation in the "here and now", I suspect there is a "there and then" time in Fiona's life when she was much younger where she learned to help others and make it better for them when they were distressed. However, we will not be going to the source of the learned behaviour and the specific moment when this role in "helping others in their distress" came into being, because we are doing a brief intervention and not a psychodynamic intervention. I decide that I need her to experience and connect with the feeling of heaviness in her body from the past which is activated in the "here and now".

The session

I frame the role analysis to her:

> Fiona, as you're showing me this scene, what I'm understanding is the following: in a situation where someone is in distress and they're making demands on you to help, you feel sad, hopeless, overwhelmed and very responsible for the other, with a belief that you should make it better and there's only you that can do this, so you're left with an enormous feeling of responsibility and you ruminate about it later.

At this point, I pick up my rucksack, which contains papers, books and my computer, and pass it to her to hold. "This represents the kind of heaviness in your body, the responsibility that you end up carrying around with you." She is still in the manager chair, and I have chosen my rucksack as a prop to represent responsibility because the body has a memory and Fiona maybe "experiencing" the heaviness here, and I want to help her to understand where the feelings come from (Gendlin 1997; Rothschild 2000). She looks surprised as I give her the bag to hold, and I repeat the role analysis emphasising the word "responsibility" and pointing to the rucksack and ask her, "Is this feeling of heaviness and responsibility familiar?"

After a moment she whispers, "Oh my God, yes! It's my mum!" Pause. A longer pause ... she repeats, "It's my mum." She looks at me. "I can't believe this," she continues, "my parents divorced ... when I was young, I am an only child ... and I always felt I had to make it better for both my parents." Pause. "That's incredible, I can't believe it, the link ... I just didn't see it. I always had this feeling that I was responsible."

My thinking

Fiona is having a moment of action-insight (Kellerman 1992), recognising where she learnt that she "should" be able to do something and the feeling of being responsible. This feeling had a heavy quality to it because it was a burden she continued to carry around if the same triggers were activated.

The jigsaw puzzle was complete, and I believe the role analysis had done its job and helped me to understand Fiona's response to others' distress in the work situation.

Overdeveloped and underdeveloped roles

I had no intention of focusing on Fiona's past life, I was here to help her with the current situation, and it was evident there was a role conflict here, there was a part of her management role which was underdeveloped, namely the ability to offer a compassionate detachment with claimants and to support her team by delegating work at this particular time of the flooding, but to also understand that she was not the only person in the team who had to take the whole responsibility for the claimants. The conflict, as far as I could see, was her overdeveloped role of the sensitive manager (a version of the sensitive daughter role), believing only she could do something to save the claimant and excluding the rest of her team (Clayton 1994; Daniel 2007).

The session: manage the internal conflict

We have about 15 minutes left, so I ask her, "Where does that responsibility need to go?" She is still sitting in the manager chair holding the rucksack. My thinking at this point is to help her to give the responsibility back to her parents so we can move to the "here and now" role of manager and do some role training (Clayton 1994). Fiona speaks, "Well it's not really mine is it? Actually it belongs to my parents." Fiona is quick to acknowledge this, so I reply, "Well it's up to you where you want to put that responsibility (my rucksack holding the role), either in a corner, or I could write 'Parents' on paper and you can give it back to them?" She likes this idea, but I also sense she has a warmth for her parents, and because it is a brief intervention, I don't want her to feel that her parents are "bad" or I am being judgemental. To me, it is a clear case of separating the heaviness from her management role and "giving it" away to a place it belongs.

I ask:

> How would you feel about handing back the responsibility to your parents, but then taking something from them that will help you and support you in this role as a manager, which is about self-care so you can look after yourself?

Fiona's face lit up, "Yes, I like that idea." I am thinking about ego strengthening and giving her compassion for an incredibly difficult situation she is dealing with at work. I quickly write "Parents" on A4 paper and place it on the floor a good space away at the back of the two chairs. But before I go any further, I want Fiona to understand that we are going

Working with role analysis in an organisation 179

to strengthen her underdeveloped manager role, so I ask Fiona to stand up and leave responsibility on the chair of her manager role for a moment. I take her out of the action. On an A4 sheet of paper I write:

Manager: enough responsibility, self compassion, team work

I ask Fiona to hold the A4 sheet and to speak aloud the words of her new role to her old manager role sat in the chair, in order to give herself a new message. Fiona goes with it, "I do have empathy for people." I correct her and say, "Imagine your old self, being a manager getting completely overwhelmed with the work, is sitting in the chair, Fiona, and you are giving yourself a message so you will begin with, 'You do have empathy.'" Fiona has another attempt, "You do have empathy for people, but you cannot be responsible for thousands of people who have suffered in the floods because that responsibility is not all yours." At this point I ask her what she wants to do with the rucksack. "I'll put it over there with my parents," pointing to the sheet of paper with "Parents" written on it. She places the bag next to the sheet, and as she returns to her standing position of the new manager role, she picks up a soft pink ball and holds it, saying to herself, "This is for me, about self care." I ask her to speak aloud to her old manager role in the chair and to choose something that represents the team. She picks up a small scarf, and with the pink ball speaks to the empty chair that represents her old manager role, "It's a difficult time, you need to take care of yourself or else it becomes too much," and places the pink ball on the chair with the scarf and says, "You're the manager of a team, and they're a good team, they all support each other, and you need to recognise this, you cannot do it all by yourself, they've got ideas." At which point she stops, "Oh my goodness, I've just realised, they've created a whole new list that customers can access to speed up the process, so I can also suggest the claimants check this out." "Is this a new policy procedure?", I ask. "Yes, it is," and she begins to reel off policy names. I interject:

I'm just going to stop you here, Fiona, because as I mentioned earlier, I don't know about the company policies, but it seems to me you have found something through this work that you can offer the customers which you had forgotten about.

This seemed a positive move, and I could see Fiona in the here and now of the session looking lighter and smiling when she spoke.

Role training: 5 minutes

The last part of the action work is to help Fiona practise this new role with the customer, and is known as a role training scene. I want her to practise her new manager role that was previously underdeveloped. I set up the chairs again by placing her in the manager chair and saying, "We are going back to the customer telling you that she has lost her home in the floods and she has three children. Let's hear your new response." Fiona takes a deep breath and begins her response. It is succinct, helpful, and she finds her words:

> I'm sorry to hear this has happened, and we can help you, we also have a process in the company to speed up claims such as yours, people who are affected by the floods. It might be helpful to get a doctor's note, and there is a list of agencies we can give to you to support you whilst claiming.

Fiona continues explaining the next stages of the process, and I can see she is able to do this in her new manager role without the "burden of responsibility" that has weighed her down in the past and with a detached compassion. At the end of the role training scene, I ask Fiona to "de-role" the chairs and props and place them back to their original positions.

Sharing

We sit back down in our original chairs from the beginning of our session. Fiona looks lighter and is smiling, "I've never done anything like that before, it was incredible, I feel so much better, it's amazing." I hear this and think, "This is the magic of psychodrama." I usually share a little about myself in these sessions because, again, the relational aspect of the work is so important. Fiona went with the process because she trusted me during the session:

> I want to share with you, Fiona, that I too have an overdeveloped sense of responsibility in my work, and this comes from my early years when my parents divorced and I always felt I could make it better for everyone. It took me a long time to work this out, but once I understood it, then it all made sense.

We continue to share, and Fiona then talks more about the company and different training events she has attended. She is beginning to cool down from the work. As I look at the clock, we have come to the end of the session with a few minutes to spare, and I say, "OK Fiona, we need to end it here, and I wish you all the best in the future." She collects her papers and pen and walks to the door, she turns around and says: "Thank you for sharing your story, Maxine, it's been really important for me to know I'm not alone with it."

Conclusion

In this chapter, I have written about a brief intervention session with a client who attended a drop-in clinic within a corporate organisation seeking help to manage stress when faced with challenging situations. I have given the example of role analysis and role theory as a template in this session for tracking the belief system in order to make the interventions around under-developed and overdeveloped roles for the client in her management position.

References

Bustos, D.M. (1994) Wings and roots, in *Psychodrama Since Moreno* (ed. P. Holmes, M. Karp & M. Watson), London: Routledge.

Clayton, M. (1994) Role theory and its clinical application, in *Psychodrama Since Moreno* (ed. P. Holmes, M. Karp & M. Watson), London: Routledge.

Daniel, S. (2007) Psychodrama, role theory and the cultural atom: New developments in role theory, in *Psychodrama: Advances in Theory and Practice* (ed. C. Baim, M. Maciel & J. Burmeister), London: Routledge.

Gendlin, E.T. (1997) *Experiencing and the Creation of Meaning*, Evanston, IL: Northwestern University Press.

Goldman, E.E., Morrison, D.S. (1984) *Psychodrama: Experience and Process*, Dubuque, IA: Kendall/Hunt.

Jefferies, J. (2004) Where lies the danger? A psychodrama approach, in *Working with Dangerous People: The Psychopathy of Violence* (ed. D. Jones), Oxford, UK: Radcliffe Medical Press.

Kellerman, P.F. (1992) *Focus on Psychodrama: The Therapeutic Aspects of Psychodrama*, London: Jessica Kingsley.

Mearns, D., Cooper, M. (2018) *Working at Relational Depth in Counselling and Psychotherapy*, 2nd ed., London: SAGE.

Moreno, J.L. (1953) *Who Shall Survive?* 2nd ed., revised, Beacon, NY: Beacon House.

Rogers, C. (1980) Empathic: An unappreciated way of being, in *A Way of Being*, New York: Houghton Mifflin.

Rothschild, B. (2000) The body remembers: Understanding somatic memory, in *The Body Remembers: The Psychophysiology of Trauma and Trauma Treatment*, London: W.W. Norton.

Tehrani, N. (ed.) (2011) *Managing Trauma in the Workplace: Supporting Workers and Organisations*, London: Routledge.

Vaihinger, H. (1924) *The Philosophy of "As If": A System of the Theoretical, Practical and Religious Fictions of Mankind*, trans. by C.K. Ogden, London: Kegan Paul, Trench, Trubner & Co.

Young, J.E. (1999) *Cognitive Therapy for PD: A Schema-focused Approach*, 3rd ed., Sarasota, FL: Professional Resource Press.

Index

abuse 84, 102, 109, 114
action 15, 17, 25; addictions compass structure 69–73; children 95; corporate drop-in session 174–175; role taking 52; session structure 13, 14
action area 58–59, 60–61, 64, 65, 69, 95
action-insight 112, 177
active empathy 97
addictions 68–79; addictions compass structure 68–73; intergenerational addictions action genogram 73–78
adolescence 142
agency 56
aggression 27, 100, 101, 103
amygdala 130, 131, 143
Andersen, Hans Christian 105
anger 58–59, 108, 109, 131, 151, 152–153
anorexia nervosa (AN) 142–143
anxiety 130–140; eating disorders 148; grief and loss 120, 121; Lucy's case 157, 160–161; perspectives on 130–132; prevalence of 130; shame 108, 109, 113; small world concretisation 37–39
art: children 98, 99; dream work 86–87; expressionism 9; working with shame 114, 115–116
"as if" situations 15, 67; corporate drop-in session 174–175; doubling 65; dream work 81; grief and loss 123; role taking 51, 55; session structure 14; shame 114, 116
attachment 72, 135, 136, 142
attunement 15–16, 60, 128; lack of, 134, 135, 136
autonomy 26, 27

Baim, C. 135
Balint, M. 136
Bamber, James 1, 18
Bannister, Anne 94
Barlow, D. H. 130
Bateman, A. 115
Bateson, G. 24
behaviours: anxiety 134; children 101, 102; corporate drop-in session 172, 173, 176; eating disorders 145, 146, 149; grief and loss 121; London Centre approach 27, 28; role theory 24–25; shame 110–111, 113, 116
beliefs: anxiety 134; children 101, 102; corporate drop-in session 172, 173, 176; dream work 83; eating disorders 142, 145, 146–147, 150, 152; grief and loss 121, 122; life challenges 78; London Centre approach 27, 28; negative 103; role theory 25; schemas 172; shame 110, 111–112, 113, 116; small world concretisation 37, 40
bereavement 119–129
Biddle, B. J. 19
binge eating 142–143, 148, 149
Blair, Andrea 2
Blatner, Adam 22–23, 97, 113
Blatner, Allee 22–23
body, connecting with the 150–152
body dissatisfaction 142
Boury, Virginie 2, 130–140
brain 130–131, 143
"breakthrough moments" 12
brief sessions 169–181
Buber, Martin 8
bulimia nervosa (BN) 142–143, 146
bullying 153,154
Bustos, Dalmiro 17, 25–27, 28, 110

catharsis 12, 29, 58, 111–112, 124
Chesner, Anna 1–3, 7–18; addictions 68–79; concretisation 31–50; dream work 80–89; role taking 51–67
children 93–104; mother-infant relationship 106–107, 136; roles 24, 26
Chinese culture 119–120, 162
Clayton, Max 17, 23–24
closure 13, 29, 139
cognitive-behavioural therapy (CBT) 131, 132, 172
collective roles 21
communicube 33, 73, 84–85
communiwell 33, 35
compassion 110, 114, 166, 178; children 97; Compassionate Self 149, 150
concretisation 31–50, 59, 138; dream work 84–85; eating disorders 147–148; grief and loss 120, 126–128; intergenerational addictions action genogram 73–74; Lucy's case 160, 161–162; shame 112–113, 115–116
confidentiality 102
connectedness 103, 105, 107, 117, 138; see also tele
consent 15
consequences: anxiety 134; children 101, 102; corporate drop-in session 172, 173, 176; eating disorders 145, 150; grief and loss 121, 122; London Centre approach 28; role theory 25; shame 110, 111, 113, 116
containment 93, 96, 103, 135
context: anxiety 134; children 101, 102; corporate drop-in session 171, 173, 176; eating disorders 145, 149; grief and loss 121; London Centre approach 27; role theory 24–25; shame 110, 111, 112, 116
Coping Role System 23
corporate setting 169–181
countertransference 133, 151, 161
creativity 7, 17, 22, 132, 139; children 94, 103; concretisation 49; lack of 134; role theory 46
cultural atom concept 45
"cultural conserves" 7, 8, 10, 15, 17
culture 17

Daniel, S. 17
Daniels, Maxine 3, 169–181
Davies, Paula 2, 93–104

Dayton, Tian 68
de-roling 15, 53–55, 61; addictions compass structure 73; corporate drop-in session 180; grief and loss 125; intergenerational addictions action genogram 77–78; session structure 14; sharing 95; small world concretisation 42, 48
defence mechanisms 94
depression 46, 76–77, 119, 120, 130, 156
diabulimia 146
dialogue 14, 16, 51; dream work 83, 88; empty chair 122–125, 147, 153, 163, 164, 174–175, 180; internal 146–147
directors 15, 52, 58; see also therapists
dissociation 114, 131, 143, 160, 168
dissociative identity disorder (DID) 156, 159–160, 164
distance 115, 149, 164; family sculpts 45; putting experience into words 114; role taking 56; shame 112; small world concretisation 37, 126
divorce 177, 180
doubling 56–58, 65–67; addictions compass structure 72; children 96–98; containing double 116; grief and loss 125; Lucy's case 164; shame 114; touch 16
drawing 86–87, 98, 100; see also art
dreams 21, 80–89
drop-in clinic 169–181
Drucker, K. 116
drug use 74–77

eating disorders 141–155
embarrassment 108
emotions (feelings): anxiety 134; attunement 60; capacity to recognise 106; children 98, 101, 102; connecting with the body 150–151; corporate drop-in session 172, 173, 176; dream work 80–81; eating disorders 145, 150; emotional regulation 15, 17; grief and loss 120, 121, 123–125, 128; London Centre approach 27; role taking 58–59; role theory 25; shame 107–108, 110, 111–112, 113, 116
empathy 97
empty chair dialogue 122–125, 147, 153, 163, 164, 174–175, 180
encounter 8
ending therapy 154

184 Index

enmeshment 151, 152–153
experiential psychotherapy 15, 131, 143
expressionism 9

family: divorce 177, 180; giving
  responsibility back to parents 178;
  grief and loss 120; intergenerational
  addictions action genogram 73–78;
  lack of maternal attunement 134–136;
  Lucy's case 157–158, 162–164, 166;
  maternal enmeshment 151, 152–153;
  mirror technique 99; parental
  transference 163; role reversal 100;
  shame 113–114
family sculpts 45–46
feedback 73
feelings *see* emotions
Fonagy, P. 115
Fox, J. 19, 29
Fragmenting Dysfunctional Role System
  23
the frame 9–10
friendship 26–27

gender 17
genograms 73–78
Gilbert, P. 106, 114
Goldman, E. E. 68
Greek mythology 9
grief 119–129
group psychodrama 11–13, 67; action
  95; addictions 68; the double 56–58;
  dreams 80–81; Lucy's case 162,
  165–167; mirroring 98–99; role
  analysis 101; role reversal 99; sharing
  95; touch 15, 16
guilt 108, 119, 153, 165
Guntrip, H. 128

healing 29
hoarding 114, 115–116, 117, 157, 164
holding environment 128
Holmes, Paul 31
Hong Kong 119, 156
Hudgins, K. 116

identification 37
imagery 80
imagination 21, 80
impulsiveness 7
independence 26
infant-mother interaction 106–107, 136

initiator role 133, 134, 137, 139
inner world, secret 158–160, 161,
  163–164, 165–167
intergenerational addictions action
  genogram 73–78
internal dialogue 146–147
intuitive eating 144

Jefferies, Jinnie 1, 2, 18, 19–30, 145,
  171

Kafka, F. 31
Kipper, D. A. 20
Kirchner, Ernst Ludwig 9
Koumpli, Eva 2–3, 141–155

learned helplessness 107
length of sessions 10
Leutz, Grete 80–81
limbic system 143
liminal space 31
Linton, Ralph 19, 20
listening 17
locus of role 25, 26, 28, 116–117
London Centre for Psychodrama 1, 2,
  13, 27–29, 110, 133, 171
loss 119–129

Mak, Lydia 2, 119–129
marriage 22, 23
masks 161
matrix of role 25, 26
McShane, Johanna 142
Mead, George Herbert 19
medication 131
memories: anxiety 135–136, 139; dream
  work 85, 87–88; group psychodrama
  11; psychodramatic roles 21; small
  world concretisation 39
"Memory Lane" technique 43
mentalisation 40, 59, 100, 115
meta-role 113, 114
Miller, S. 107, 108
mindfulness 7, 17, 132, 149, 150
miniatures 33–49; children 95, 99, 100;
  grief and loss 120, 126–128; *see also*
  small world concretisation
mirroring 59, 63, 67, 77; anxiety
  136–137; children 96, 98–99; failures
  in 114, 115; group psychodrama 11;
  shame 114
Mollon, Phil 105

Moreno, Jacob L.: action-insight 112; children 96; connectedness 105, 117; encounter 8; expressionism 9; role taking 53; role theory 17, 19–22, 25–26, 28–29, 46, 96, 101, 109–110, 143–144; social and cultural atom concepts 45; spontaneity 7, 22, 46, 132; surgery metaphor 11; "surplus reality" 80; *tele* 46, 94, 133; warm-up 7; *Who Shall Survive?* 171
Moreno, Zerka 17, 68
Morrison, D. S. 68
mother-infant relationship 106–107, 136
mourning 119; *see also* grief
multiple perspectives 59–65

Napier, Anna 2, 105–118
narratives 42–43, 78, 144
Nathanson, D. L. 108
Nietzsche, Friedrich 154

object relations theory 131
objects 33–49, 99–100, 115–116, 138–139, 147–148; *see also* miniatures

panic attacks 131, 132, 134
parental transference 163
passivity 26
Paulson, Tony 142
personality 23
play 31, 32, 96, 101
poetry 8
power 16
Progressive Roles 23, 24
projective identification 109
Prometheus 9
protagonists: action 95; dream work 80–81; group psychodrama 11–12; mirroring 98–99; role of the double 56–58; touch 15–16
proxemics 56
psychoanalysis 10, 131
psychodrama: addictions 68–79; anxiety 130–140; children 93–104; concretisation 31–50, 112; corporate setting 169–181; creativity and spontaneity 7–8, 22; dream work 80–89; eating disorders 141–155; encounter 8; grief and loss 119–129; holism 9; Lucy's case 156–168; mentalisation 59; role taking 51–67; session length and frequency 10;

session structure 13, 14, 93–96; shame 105–118; touch 15–17; transgenerational 73; as way of thinking 17–18; *see also* group psychodrama
psychodramatic roles 21, 145
psychological hygiene 52
psychosomatic roles 21, 145
psychotherapy: addictions 68; authenticity and experimentation 65; children 93–104; the frame 9–10; grief and loss 120; play 31, 32; touch 15; *see also* group psychodrama
puppets 95, 98, 99, 100
Putnam, F. W. 159

reflection 16, 17; addictions compass structure 73; dream work 81, 85; role taking 67; sharing 95–96; small world concretisation 37, 42
relationships: "as if" experiments 51; concretisation 45–46; eating disorders 141–142; group psychodrama 11; Lucy's case 161, 163, 165, 166–167, 168; mother-infant relationship 106–107; role taking 53, 59; role theory 23; social roles 144
Resch, E. 144
resilience 93, 103
responsibility, taking 78
rivalry 26–27
role: addictions compass structure 69–72; anxiety 132–134, 139; children 95; concretisation 46–49; corporate drop-in session 178–179; dream work 83–84, 87, 88; as encounter with the other 55–59; group psychodrama 16; intergenerational addictions action genogram 73–74, 77–78; Lucy's case 167; meta-role 113, 114; shame 105, 106, 109–110, 113, 116–117; types of roles 21; *see also* role reversal; role taking; role theory; role training
role analysis 17, 28; anxiety 133, 139; children 93, 101–103; corporate drop-in session 171–172, 173, 176–177, 178; dream work 83, 88; eating disorders 145–146, 149–150; grief and loss 121–122; group psychodrama 11; life challenges 78; shame 110–111, 114, 116, 117

role clarity 10, 52
role perception 20
role playing 20
"role reciprocity" 22
role repertoires 8, 21, 46, 96, 105–106, 164
role reversal 59, 65; anxiety 133, 135; children 96, 99–100; corporate drop-in session 175; dream work 81, 83–84; eating disorders 147, 148, 152; grief and loss 123–125, 127, 128; group psychodrama 16; Lucy's case 160, 161–162, 163–164; multiple perspectives 59; shame 112, 113; small world concretisation 37
role taking 37, 48, 51–67, 126
role theory 17, 19–30, 96; concretisation 46, 49; eating disorders 143–145; shame 106, 109–110, 117
role training 23–24, 29; corporate drop-in session 179–180; dream work 81; group psychodrama 11; Lucy's case 162, 164

safety 15
sand trays 33, 35
Sartre, Jean-Paul 106
scale 87
scene setting 82, 147–148
schemas 172
Schön, Donald 17
Schore, A. N. 107
Schützenberger, Anne Ancelin 73
secret inner world 158–160, 161, 163–164, 165–167
self: addictions compass structure 71–72; Compassionate Self 149, 150; development of sense of 106–107; dream work 80, 85; Lucy's case 167–168; role theory 19, 24, 143–144; small world concretisation 37; Wise Self 72, 73
self-criticism 110, 111, 113, 120, 134, 148, 149
self-disclosure 95, 180
self-harm 46, 120, 122, 146
self-regulation 107, 150
separation 139
session length and frequency 10
session structure 13, 14, 93–96

shame 105–118; eating disorders 141, 148, 149, 154; grief and loss 125
sharing 12, 16, 95–96, 180
small world concretisation 33–49; children 95, 99, 100; dream work 84–85; grief and loss 126–128; intergenerational addictions action genogram 73–74
social atom concept 45, 160
social roles 21, 144
sociodrama 9
sociometry 9, 20, 94
somatic roles 21, 144
space 17, 56; action area 58–59, 60–61, 64, 65, 69, 95; intergenerational addictions action genogram 73–74; see also distance
spectograms 99, 120, 126–128, 160; see also miniatures
spontaneity 7–8, 17, 22, 132, 137–138; children 94, 96, 103; initiator role 139; lack of 134; role theory 46; sand trays 33; small world concretisation 48
stage 33, 51, 81
status nascendi 25, 26, 28
stories 95, 98, 99, 100
Stossel, S. 130, 131
suicidal ideation 120, 121–122, 123, 125, 126–128
"surplus reality" 49, 80, 81, 125

Tang, Esther 3, 156–168
tangle metaphor 12–13, 17
tele 46, 94, 133
therapeutic relationship 128; children 93, 94, 103; eating disorders 145–146, 151, 154; the frame 9–10; grief and loss 125; Lucy's case 160; power asymmetry 16; shame 117; transference 17
therapists: doubling 58; dream work 81, 88; multiple perspectives 59–65; touch 15–16; use of role 51; see also directors
third space 31
Thomas, E. J. 19
timelines 42–44, 160
touch 15–17
transference 17, 37–42, 163
transgenerational psychodrama 73

trauma: children 94, 96;
eating disorders 141–142, 152–153;
ending therapy 154; experiential
psychotherapy 143; intergenerational
addictions action genogram 78;
psychodramatic roles 145;
secondary 173; shame 110, 114,
116–117; transgenerational
psychodrama 73
Tribole, E. 144

Van der Kolk, Bessel 143

warm-up 7; children 93–94; group
psychodrama 11; role taking 52, 53,
56; session structure 13, 14
Williams, Anthony 17, 24–25, 26, 27, 28,
43, 103, 110
Winnicott, D. 31, 32, 106–107
Wise Self 72, 73
women 142
working through 15
Wurmser, L. 108

Young, J. E. 172

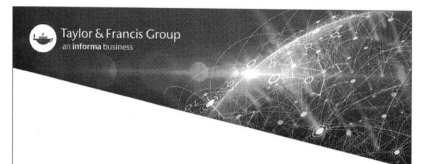